Obilson A. Ruiz

In Detail 1

English for Global Communication

Isobel Rainey de Diaz

with

Kristin L. Johannsen

THOMSON

HEINLE

United States · Australia · Canada · Mexico · Singapore · Spain · United Kingdom

THOMSON
HEINLE

In Detail 1
Isobel Rainey de Diaz

Publisher: *Chris Wenger*
Editorial Manager: *Berta de Llano*
Senior Development Editor: *Jean Pender*
Development Editor: *Ivor Williams*
Sr. Production Editor: *Sally Cogliano*
Executive Marketing Manager: *Amy Mabley*
Manufacturing Coordinator: *Mary Beth Hennebury*
Cover Image: *"Digital Highway" by Todd Davidson*
Compositor: *Graphic World*

Project Manager: *Kris Swanson*
Photography Manager: *Sheri Blaney*
Illustrator: *Raketshop*
Cover Designer: *Joseph Sherman*
Interior Designer: *Jean Hammond*
Printer: *Transcontinental*
Also participating in the publication of this program were:
Editorial: *Sean Birmingham, Paul MacIntyre, Stephanie Schmidt, Carmen Corral-Reid*
Marketing: *Ian Martin, John Lowe, Francisco Lozano, Helena Nagano*

For permission to use material from this text or product contact us:
Tel   1-800-730-2214
Fax   1-800-730-2215
Web   www.thomsonrights.com

0-8384-4530-6
Photo Credits
2: Christian Peacock/ISI; **4:** Richard Kasmier/ISI; **6:** c: Lee Paterson/ISI; b. Minnesota Historical Society/CORBIS; **7:** l. to r.: Stewart Cohen/ISI; Bruce Buchanan/ISI; Todd Powell/ISI; Chuck Carlton/ISI; Mark Segal/ISI; **10:** Bill Bachmann/ISI; **11:** clockwise: Reuters NewMedia Inc./CORBIS; Peter Turnley/CORBIS; Reuters; NewMedia, Inc./CORBIS; Wally McNamee/CORBIS; **12:** Omni Photo Communications Inc./ ISI; **13:** SW Productions/ISI; **14:** PhotoDisc/Getty Images; **16:** t., both: Benelux Press/ISI; b.: Volvox/ISI; **18:** l.: Pam Ostrow/ISI; **20:** l.: Rock Souders/ISI; **21:** clockwise: © Reuters NewMedia Inc./CORBIS; © Reuters NewMedia, Inc./CORBIS; © CORBIS; © CORBIS; **22:** © Michael S. Yamashita/CORBIS; **23:** clockwise: © Denis O'Regan/CORBIS; © Mitchell Gerber/CORBIS; © Tim Mosenfelder/CORBIS; **24:** t. to b.: Kindra Clineff/ISI; David Ball/ISI; Bob Burch/ISI; **26:** © Bettmann/CORBIS; **29:** Agencia Estado Ltda, Brasil; **30:** l. to r.: Zephyr Picture/ISI; SW Production/ISI; Chip Henderson/ISI; Greig Cranna/ISI; **33:** Spike and Ethel/ISI; **36:** Ahn Young-Joon/AP; **37:** l.: Stewart Cohen/ISI; r.: Duomo/CORBIS; **39:** l to r.: © AFP/CORBIS; Art Rickerby/TimePix; Hulton/Getty; **40:** James Lafayette/ISI; **41:** (Duomo/CORBIS; **43:** © Reuters NewMedia Inc./CORBIS; **44:** t. to b.: elektraVision/ISI; AFP/CORBIS; Reuters NewMedia/CORBIS; Reuters NewMedia Inc./CORBIS; bottom right: © Reuters NewMedia Inc./CORBIS; **45:** clockwise: PhotoDisc/Getty; Frank Staub/ISI; Inga Spence/ISI; Evan Roberts/AURORA Photos; **46:** William Holdman/ISI; **47:** Walter Bibikow/ISI; **50:** Mark Culbertson/ISI; **54:** © Spencer Grant/Photo Edit; **56:** t. to b.: © Mike Johnson/Earth Window; Elizabeth DeLaney/ISI; PhotoDisc/Getty Images; **57:** Bill Romerhaus/ISI; **62:** © Jose Luis Pelaez/CORBIS; **64:** t. to b.: PhotoDisc/Getty; **69:** clockwise: © Roy Botterell/CORBIS; © Chris Hellier/CORBIS; © Paul A. Souders/CORBIS; Derek Cole/ISI; © Jim Erickson/CORBIS; **74:** l.to r.: Steve Dunwell Photography Inc./ISI; Frank Siteman/ISI; Fotopic/ISI; Dan Gair Photographic/ISI; b: © CORBIS; **76:** © Tony Freeman/Photo Edit; **79:** clockwise: Rudi Von Briel/ISI; RF/CORBIS; Barbara Benner/ISI; Derek Trask/RF/CORBIS; **80:** Terry Why/ISI; **81:** Inga Spence/ISI; 82: Walter Bibikow/ISI; **84:** tl.:Bob Burch/ISI; tr.: Erwin Nielsen/ISI; b.: © Bettmann/CORBIS; **86:** l. to r.: ageFOTOSTOCK AMERICA INC.; Bill Lai/ISI; Bruce Leighty/ISI; Kindra Clineff/ISI; b.: PhotoDisc/Getty Images; **87:** Cat/ISI; Rick Strange/ISI; **88:** l. to r.: Kindra Clineff/ISI; David Ball/ISI; Bob Burch/ISI; **90:** © Bettmann/CORBIS; **94:** l. to r.: The Kobal Collection/Mirabai Films/Delhi Dot Com; The Kobal Collection/Film Workshop; The Kobal Collection/El Deseo/Renn/France 2; **95:** both: © Bettmann/CORBIS; **98:** l.: © Jeremy Hormer/CORBIS; r.: © AFP/CORBIS; **103:** clockwise: James Smalley/ISI; Peter Walton/ISI; Jeff Greenberg/ISI; © 2002 PhotoDisc/Getty Images **108:** l.: Gary Conner/ISI; center top: John Dominis/ISI; center bottom: Ed Lallo/ISI; r.: Chip Henderson/ISI; **110:** © Superstock; **112:** t.: Reuters NewMedia Inc./CORBIS; l.: Walter Bibikow/ISI; r.: Michael Keller/ISI; **113:** t.: SW Production/ISI; Kathleen Kliskey-Geraghty/ISI; b.: Edward Slater/ISI; **114:** t.: EyeWire/Getty Images; r.: PhotoDisc/Getty Images; b.: PhotoDisc Getty Images; **118:** PhotoDisc/Getty Images; **119:** Cleo Freelance/ISI; **123:** clockwise: © David Young-Wolff/Photo Edit; The Kobal Collection/Steven Bochco Productions/Timothy White; © David Young-Wolff/Photo Edit; The Kobal Collection/Paul Drinkwater; **124:** t.: AFP/CORBIS; b.: Benelux Press/ISI; **127:** t.: © hulton-Deutsch/CORBIS; rest: © Bettmann/CORBIS; **129:** © Getty Images; **130:** t.: Paul Meyer/ISI; ctr.: Gary Conner/ISI;
Text Credits
Page 114: "Everybody Needs Someone" by Helen Steiner Rice, © 1971 The Helen Steiner Rice Foundation—All Rights Reserved; Used with permission of The Helen Steiner Rice Foundation, Cincinnati, Ohio; "My Friendship" by Emily Ryon, © 2003; **Page 115:** "The Guy in the Glass" by Peter Dale Wimbrow, © 1934 Dale Wimbrow; **Page 121:** "Family and Friends" by Bonnie Best, © 1999; "Water Jar Cracks" by Basho

Author's Acknowledgments

While writing this series, the author was Visiting ESP Lecturer in the Escuela Universitaria de Ingeniería Técnica Minera at the University of León, Spain. She would like to express her gratitude to the Director of the School Don Fernando Fernández San Elías for his encouragement, and for the confidence he showed her in allowing her access to her office at the weekends. She is also indebted to the Director of Studies Don Gustavo Elízaga Antón for his practical support, and to all her colleagues, administrative staff, teachers and students, in the School for their cheerful cooperation inside and outside the classroom.

The author also wishes to acknowledge that, while writing the series, her family—Pedro Agustín, Julian, Ivan, Jan and Jo—have been a major source of inspiration and fortitude.

Sincere thanks are also due to the editorial team Berta, Jean, and Ruth and support author Kristin for their singleminded determination not just to produce a wonderful upper intermediate/advanced series but to get it published on schedule!

In addition to the above, we would like to extend our thanks to the following professionals who have offered invaluable comments and suggestions during the development of this series:

Nicolas Baychelier, *Chung Yuan Christian University, Taiwan*

Andrew Berriman, *Shih Hsin University, Taiwan*

Grazyna Anna Bonomi, *Yázigi Internexus, Brasil*

An-Jean Chiang, *Yuan Ze University, Taiwan*

Tania Cvihun Kedzior, *ITESM Prepa Tec Eugenio Garza Sada, México*

Tamaki Harrold, *Simul Academy, Japan*

Margaret B. Hug, *ESL Specialist Program, U.S. Consulate, México*

Patricia Lalange del Vall, *Instituto de Enseñanza Superior del Ejército, Argentina*

Patricia Alejandra Lastiri, *Instituto de Enseñanza Superior del Ejército, Argentina*

Han-yi Lin, Language Center, *National Cheng-chi University, Taiwan*

Ramiro Luna Rivera, *ITESM, México*

Maria Teresa Maiztegui, *Uniao Cultural Brasil Estados Unidos, Brasil*

Claudia Marín Cabrera, *Comunidad Educativa Diocesana El Buen Pastor / Pontificia Universidad Católica del Peru*

Maria Ordoñez, *Universidad de Celaya, México*

Stephen Shrader, *Language Institute of Japan*

Kang-Jen Tien, *Chang-Gung University, Taiwan*

Maria Christina Uchoa Close, *Instituto Cultural Brasil-Estados Unidos, Brasil*

Table of Contents

Fashion

Communication

Discussing appearance and style

Asking for and giving opinions

Evaluating products

Grammar

Verbs and expressions with the
   –ing form

Vocabulary

Fads and fashions

Appearance and dress

Compound adjectives

Skills

Reading for specific information:
   newspaper column

Listening using background
   knowledge

Writing a magazine or newspaper
   report

1   Warm Up

A. PAIR WORK Describe the pictures in as much detail as possible. Talk about the people's clothes and hair styles. Where are they and what are they doing? What sort of people are they?

B. Put the words and expressions under the appropriate heading.

> sneakers   boots   miniskirts   sweat shirts   T-shirts   chinos   flared pants
> jeans   long hair for men   long hair for women   shaved head for men or
> women   dreadlocks   jogging   skateboarding   hip-hop dancing   playing
> computer games   bungee jumping

C. PAIR WORK Use the words in each group to talk about what is in or out of fashion in your country.

EXAMPLES:

> *Hip-hop dancing is in and jogging is out.*
> *Sneakers are out and boots are in*
>   *this year.*
> *Jeans are always in fashion.*

FYI
We usually say
something is "in" or "out"
instead of in fashion
and out of fashion.

Out of fashion	In fashion	Always in fashion

Dealing with unfamiliar words in a reading

When you are reading a long text, you will not understand every single word. Do not worry about this. You can still understand most of the text, even when you do not know exactly what every word means.

Before you read

A. How important is fashion to you? How and where do you find out about the latest fashions in clothes and hair styles? What do you think is the difference between a fad and a fashion?

First reading

B. Read the text and complete the lists of fads and fashions mentioned.

FYI

fad = an activity that people go wild about for a time (The word *craze* is also used.)

Fads	Fashions in clothes
1. _____	1. hot pants
2. skateboarding	2. _____
3. _____	3. _____

Fads and Fashions

My mother, who is seventy-six, was clearing out her attic last week, and horror of
5 horrors, she came across some of the clothes I wore as a teenager in the 70s. Anyway, when my 17-year-old daughter Tanya,
10 who happened to be around at the time, saw all these old items of clothing and footwear, she was thrilled. This morning she came down to breakfast wearing a maroon tank top covered in
15 orange stars. I sure hope my mother threw out those pink hot pants!

It's true what they say: What goes around, comes around, and especially in the world of fads and fashions. Establishing a clear distinction° between fads and
20 fashions is pretty easy. A fad is an activity, like bungee jumping, that people go wild about for a while. Then the novelty wears off°, people get bored, the fad dies out, and everyone moves on to the next craze. Fashions are more about personal style—the kind of clothes you
25 wear or the way you wear your hair: dreadlocks, Afro, flattop, beehive, etc. Most fads and fashions are here today, gone tomorrow, although with the help of clever marketing people, some things come back into fashion after having been "out" for some time. However, some
30 fads or fashions have staying power, that is, they remain popular and eventually become a permanent part of our culture and lifestyle. Skateboarding, once just a fad, is now a permanent pastime in many countries. Or the miniskirt: In the 60s it was very
35 "trendy"—as people used to say back then—but it went out of fashion in the 70s. Then, in the late 80s and early 90s, it made a comeback and it looks as if it's here to stay.

These days a major cause of parent-teenager
40 clashes is the latest fad for body piercing. My friends—the parents—tell their kids that it can be dangerous. The know-it-all kids counter this by informing their poor, ignorant parents that many ancient cultures practiced body piercing. They explain
45 how the Maya pierced their tongues and Egyptian pharaohs pierced their navels°; in fact, it was a sign of courage. Of course, today's kids have to go one better than Ramses III, so they have their lips, earlobes,

eyebrows, nostrils, you name it, pierced. Tanya is
50 thinking about having something done, but she won't tell me exactly what or exactly where! I've told her to think carefully about it, and to talk to friends who have had the experience and ask them about how much it hurts and how long it takes to heal.
55   Like fads, fashions can change quickly, although some clothes, such as jeans, which we all have in our wardrobe°, never go out of fashion. Often, however, basic classics like jeans are made more upbeat by adding details such as studs° or patches. Adding a famous name
60 to the label on the jeans is another way of making them more attractive to the buyer. These "designer jeans" are not very different from ordinary jeans: they are made of the same fabric and they look similar. They just happen to cost up to $300 a pair! Most of us like to follow
65 fashion up to a point, but only a few people can afford to pay that much. Personally, I wouldn't dream of paying

such a high price for a pair of jeans. It makes me wonder where people get
70 that kind of cash. Maybe they sell off their old 70s clothes. Hey, that's it! Excuse me while I make a quick call to my mother.
75 I've got to catch her before she gives away all those platform shoes!

establishing a clear distinction = clarifying the difference between two things
the novelty wears off = something is no longer new or interesting
navel = the little hollow or protruberance in the abdomen
wardrobe = all the clothes a person owns
studs = decorative metal buttons

Second reading

C. Find these facts.

1. In what way are fads and fashions different?
2. What two things do fads and fashions have in common?
3. Which fad and which fashion mentioned in the text have become permanent in many countries?
4. Why did the Maya and the Egyptian pharaohs pierce their bodies?
5. In what way are designer jeans different from ordinary jeans?

Think about it

1. Why might people get bored with a fad?
2. Why might fads and fashions come back into fashion after they have been out of fashion for some time?
3. Why can body piercing be dangerous?
4. How does the fashion industry succeed in making money out of basic classics?

Vocabulary in context

D. Read the text again and find the following words and expressions.

1. In paragraph 2, another way to express the idea *make a comeback* (line 37) _____
2. In paragraph 2, an expression with the opposite meaning of *dies out* (line 30) _____
3. In paragraph 3, a word with the opposite meaning of *know-it-all* (line 43) _____
4. In paragraph 4, a word with a similar meaning to *upbeat* (line 61) _____

Discussion

E. GROUP WORK Discuss the fads and fashions that are popular in your country at the moment. Which of these fads and fashions would you do, wear, or have? Which would you never dream of doing, wearing, or having?

     Give reasons. Do the fashions suit you? Why or why not? Are the fads dangerous, silly, harmless, or fun?

Uses of the *-ing* form

| have dreadlocks |
| learn hip-hop dancing |
| buy designer clothes |
| play computer games |
| scuba dive   play Frisbee |
| wear miniskirts |
| surf the Internet |

Practice

A. Complete the sentence with the *-ing* form of the verb.

walk	wear	pay	rent	shop	play	try

EXAMPLE: <u>*Renting*</u> *videos became popular in the 1980s.*

1. _____ flowered shirts was very fashionable in the 1970s.
2. _____ for expensive clothes is one of her pastimes.
3. In my opinion, _____ $300 for a pair of jeans is crazy.
4. According to some doctors, _____ is better for your health than many other forms of exercise, such as weight training.
5. _____ to fit as many people as possible into a VW Beetle was a popular fad in the 1960s.
6. _____ frisbee is an old fad that makes a comeback from time to time.

B. Use gerunds (*-ing* form) to complete the sentences with true information about you and fads and fashions such as the following. Add your reason.

EXAMPLE: *I'm nervous about* <u>*shaving my head*</u>. <u>*My girlfriend won't like it*</u>.

1. I'm really interested in _____.
2. I'm afraid of _____.
3. I got tired of _____.
4. I'm very careful about _____.
5. I could never get used to _____.
6. I could never get excited about _____.
7. I look forward to _____.
8. I would never dream of _____.

C. PAIR WORK Use expressions above to talk about fads and fashions with your partner.

EXAMPLE: **You:** *I'd never dream of wearing a miniskirt.*
          Your partner: *Really? Why?*
              You: *Miniskirts don't look good on me.*

| interview   visit   go   eat |
| buy   drive   see   shop |

D. Complete the statements on the left with the gerund of one of these verbs. Then match them with the reasons on the right.

EXAMPLE: *I miss* <u>*playing Frisbee.*</u> *It was such fun.*

1. I avoid _____ on Saturdays.
2. They dislike _____ home at 6:30 p.m.
3. They quit _____ designer clothes.
4. We had trouble _____ the models.
5. He appreciated _____ more of his kids.
6. She suggested _____ to the fashion show.
7. He can't help _____ so much.
8. She enjoys _____ her grandmother.

a. She simply loves clothes.
b. They were such fun.
c. The traffic is very heavy.
d. He simply loves food.
e. They were so busy.
f. She's so funny.
g. There are always so many people.
h. They are too expensive.

Uses of the –ing form

Rule	Examples
1. A gerund is the *-ing* form of a verb.	swim—*swimming*, dance—*dancing* study—*studying*, read—*reading*
2. A gerund can be the subject of a sentence.	*Dancing* is good for your health. *Going* to the movies is fun.
3. A gerund can be the object of a verb + a preposition or a verb phrase + a preposition.	be afraid of, get used to, be careful about, be interested in, get excited about, get bored with, get tired of, look forward to, be good at, be nervous about, talk about Some people are afraid of *getting* married. I'm looking forward to *seeing* you soon.
4. A gerund can be the object of certain verbs.	avoid, delay, discuss, dislike, enjoy, finish, miss, practice, quit, have trouble, regret, spend time Some students avoid *taking* tests. He regrets *leaving* his job.

Test yourself

E. Complete the dialog with the *–ing* form of the verbs in the box.

find	include	leave out	look at	publish	read	write

Editor: Have you finished (1) publishing that report on the fashion show?

Reporter: Er . . . no, not yet. I'm having a little trouble with the text. In fact, I was thinking of (2) _____ the text completely.

Editor: What?

Reporter: Well, I think, when it's a report of a fashion show, most people enjoy (3) _____ the photos of the models much more than actually (4) _____ a report. I know I do, and I'm a writer!

Editor: Yes, you are a writer and that's what we pay you to do!

Reporter: But don't you think that (5) _____ all the photos plus a lot of text would make the report too long?

Editor: No, I don't think so. Anyway, I wouldn't dream of (6) _____ a report of a fashion show with no text. This is a respectable news magazine! Now get busy!

Reporter: Okay, boss. I'll get on it right away.

Editor: Good. I look forward to (7) _____ your report on my desk by the end of the day.

4 Speaking

Speaking focus

Asking for and giving opinions

What do you think of ...?
What's your opinion about ...? How do you feel about ...?

Personally, I think ... It seems to me ... As far as I'm concerned, ...

FYI

These expressions are often used when talking informally about fashion: I'm not into it.   It's not me.   That's not my style.

A. PAIR WORK Look at the picture and talk with your partner about the fashions that are shown. Use the expressions in the box. Then talk about new fashions you have seen in your country recently.

B. GROUP WORK Choose one of the situations below and with your group members, decide your roles. Think about what you might say to explain your opinion and persuade the other group members to agree. Make short notes. Then practice your conversation. When you're ready, take turns acting out your role plays for the class.

1. | **A:** You are a teenager and you want to color your hair bright red.
   | **B:** You are A's mother. You think A's natural hair color looks very nice.
   | **C:** You are A's friend. You think A worries about fashion too much.

2. | **A:** You are the manager of the most expensive department store in your city. You want all your employees to dress formally.
   | **B:** You are a salesperson in the department store. You have just had your hair done in a very unusual style and you really like it.
   | **C:** You are B's coworker. You think that styles are important because they show our personality.

3. | **A:** You are a 40-year-old mother or father, and your hair is getting gray. You want to color it so you can look young again.
   | **B:** You are A's teenage son or daughter. You think people shouldn't try to hide their age.
   | **C:** You are A's hairdresser. You want people to have fun with new styles.

C. Discuss the role plays with the class. Who had some interesting ideas? Do you agree or disagree with them?

Jeans first became popular in the U.S. during the California Gold Rush of the mid-nineteenth century when a German immigrant, Levi Strauss, started making hard-wearing practical pants from a fabric he brought from Germany. He called the pants Levi's. In 2002, the Levi's company paid approximately $44,000 for the oldest-known pair of jeans dating back to the 1880s. They were originally owned by a Nevada miner. Five hundred replicas of the pair were made, and they sold at $400 each.

1

2

3

4

5

badly dressed
overdressed
casually dressed
appropriately dressed
well dressed

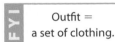

FYI Outfit =
a set of clothing.

A. Use words from the box to describe the pictures.

EXAMPLE: *The woman in picture 5 is overdressed.*

B. Read the description below. Then put the words in italics in the correct column to complete the chart.

The woman in picture 1 is well dressed. The outfit she has chosen is *simple* but *elegant* and the colors and *style* suit her. Her *accessories*—purse and shoes—*go well with* her suit, which is *beautifully cut.*

Talking about clothes

Nouns	Verbs	Adjectives	Compound adjectives
the (1) _____ = the design and overall look of clothes	to suit someone = look good on someone	casual	well dressed
(2) _____ = gloves, shoes, etc.	to (3) _____ = look good together	(4) _____ = not flashy	well made
the cut of the clothes	to match = be the same color or style as	drab = dull	well finished
A classic suit		(5) _____ = stylish	beautifully finished
		scruffy = untidy and not very clean	(6) _____
			badly made
			badly cut

C. Now use expressions from the chart to describe the people in the other pictures above.

D. PAIR WORK Would you dress like the people in the pictures?

EXAMPLES:
  S1: *Would you dress like the woman in picture 1?*
  S2: *No, it's not me. I'm not into suits. And those colors don't look good on me.*

  S1: *How about dressing like the man in picture 4?*
  S2: *You gotta be kidding! He's so scruffy!*

Listening strategy

Using background knowledge

Before you listen, consider what you already know about the topic to help you predict the ideas that you might hear.

Before you listen

A. PAIR WORK Talk about these questions with your partner.

1. Look at the labels on three things you are wearing or carrying, for example: sweater, backpack, shoes. Where were they made? If they were made overseas, what do you know about those countries? What kinds of products are made there?

2. Would you like to work in the factory that made these products? Why or why not?

3. You are going to listen to an interview about the problems of some factory workers. With your partner, list three problems that you might hear about.

First listening

B. Listen to the interview. Circle problems on your list that the speakers talked about.

Second listening

C. Listen again and find the information.

A definition of the term sweatshop	_____
Examples of bad conditions	1. _____
	2. _____
	3. _____
A solution that won't work	_____
Why not?	_____
A solution that could work	_____
Why?	_____
A good place to get information	_____

D. PAIR WORK Compare your answers with your partner and add any information you missed.

After listening

E. GROUP WORK What do you think about sweatshops? Do you think "ethical shopping" is practical? Why or why not?

Test yourself

F. You are going to hear a conversation comparing two T-shirts. Listen and answer.

1. Where are the speakers?
   a. a department store   **b.** a factory   **c.** a market   **d.** a school

2. Which brand does the man prefer?
   a. Gold Star   **b.** SOS   **c.** Blue Moon   **d.** Award

3. What is the difference in prices?
   a. $2   **b.** $4   **c.** $6   **d.** $8

7 Writing

Writing a magazine or newspaper report

Before you write

A. GROUP WORK Complete this report using one of the words or expressions in the box and other information where necessary.

beautifully cut and brightly colored	just as elegant as
badly designed and very unattractive	almost as attractive as
classical and well made	just as unattractive and badly designed as
drab colors and coarse fabrics	get a job in an office
baggy Bermudas and floppy sun hats	get a job in a gym
fabulous colors and fine fabrics	get a job in an airline

The Evening News   14

Fashion Scout

All the big names in the fashion world gathered last night at the Plaza Hotel for the much-anticipated preview of next summer's ready-to-wear fashions. All the big brand names were represented (a) _____ . *(Choose and insert three brand names.)* But I have to say I found the show more than a little disappointing. Most of the clothes were (b) _____ . *(Give a general reason to justify the writer's disappointment.)* For women, what's "in" for the summer is boring. We saw long skirts to the ankle in (c) _____ . *(Complete the reason for the author's disappointment.)* And as for men, well, don't hold your breath. The latest thing in store for you guys is (d) _____ . *(Choose and insert two items.)* The only highlight of the show for me was the sportswear, but not because of the sportswear itself. This was (e) _____ *(Compare the sportswear with the other clothes,)* the other clothes. No, it was the way they presented the clothes. Various models wearing shorts and crop tops, did great hip-hop dance routines, which brought some welcome relief after seeing all the tedious new designs on show. Maybe these models should think about a career change and (f) _____ . *(Suggest an alternative and appropriate occupation.)* But I bet they make more money as models, don't you?

Write

B. GROUP WORK In the same groups, use the following outline to write a report about an imaginary fashion show you all enjoyed. Use a separate sheet of paper to write your report.

Introduction to the report: Give season, name, place, and participants
Evaluation: Positive
General reason: Give general reason for positive evaluation
Specific reasons: Give specific reasons, mention the clothes for men and women
One disappointing aspect: *Excessive use of fads in the show, e.g. rollerblading*
Result of disappointing aspect: *e.g. Too fast—couldn't see the clothes properly*
Recommendation: *e.g. Have a separate show for fads*

A. Work with the class and brainstorm all the information you have about the four most popular brand names in your country and write them in column 1. Then brainstorm their most popular products and complete columns 2 and 3.

EXAMPLE:

Brand name	Products	Evaluation of products
Trackers	classic, casual pants and shirts for men and women	very comfortable not at all expensive stylish, but not very fashionable

B. PAIR WORK Discuss your opinions of the products and reasons for your opinions. Do you know if the companies that produce the products have fair pay and good working conditions?

EXAMPLES:

S1: What do you think of (insert brand name)_____ clothes?
S2: They're really comfortable. I enjoy wearing them.
S1: Yeah, me, too, and they're not expensive at all. What about (insert brand name) _____ footwear?
S2: I wouldn't dream of buying (insert brand name)_____shoes!
S1: Oh, why not?
S2: They're much too expensive and I've heard (insert brand name) _____uses sweatshops.
S1: That's not true. I saw a documentary about their factories, and their workers have excellent working conditions.
S2: Hmmm . . .

C. Have a general discussion with the class about the strengths and weaknesses of the products and the companies.

D. CLASS TASK Choose a famous person in your country—from the world of sports, politics, TV, or fashion—and discuss what you like and dislike about the way that person dresses, wears his or her hair, etc. Then give the person a completely new look. What kind of clothes would you choose for him or her? What hair style? As you make your decisions, draw a picture of this person on the board.

For more about travel, view the CNN video. Activities to accompany the video begin on page 137.

Couples

Communication

Discussing relationships

Asking for and giving reasons

Giving advice

Grammar

Relative clauses: restrictive and
  nonrestrictive

Vocabulary

Love and relationships

Personal qualities and problems

Three-word verbs

Skills

Reading for main ideas, facts,
  and inference: magazine
  article

Listening for sequence words

Writing a letter giving advice

1   Warm Up

A. PAIR WORK Answer the questions about the couples in the pictures.

- What are their names and occupations?
- What do you know about their marriages?
- When did they get married?
- Did their marriages survive?
- If not, when and why did they get divorced or separated?
- Did any of these couples have to face serious problems in their marriages and still stay together?
- What were the problems and why do you think they stayed together?

B. PAIR WORK Look at the word box and match the verbs on the left with the prepositions on the right. Then use the verbs to talk about the relationships or marriages of people you know about.

EXAMPLE:

    *A: Did you hear that Julia has fallen in love
       again?*
    B: Oh, no! Not again! Who is it this time?

 FYI | to break up = to end a relationship

be attracted	
break up	
fall in love	
get / be married	to
get / be engaged	with
get / be divorced	from
get / be separated	
have a relationship	
make / be friends	

Before you read

A. GROUP WORK Say whether you agree or disagree with the statements and why.

- Couples should try to do most things together.
- Couples should have the same tastes in everything: friends, clothes, food, etc.
- Falling in love is easy; staying in love is hard.
- There is no such thing as romantic love.

Reading strategy

Thinking ahead before you start reading

Think about what information you expect to find in the text. Look at the title. This usually helps you to predict the content of the text.

First reading

B. Read the paragraphs and decide which paragraph contains the information.

1. some of the characteristics of true love _____
2. problems with romantic love _____
3. one way in which celebrity couples express their togetherness _____

Why Couples Stay Together

All the celebrity couples are doing it—wearing identical outfits. Madonna and her husband Guy Ritchie, for example, were recently pictured in matching baggy° pants and flip-flops, and Ronan Keating and his
5 wife Yvonne went to a party dressed in suits which were exactly the same color and style. Hollywood's most enthusiastic wardrobe clones, however, are Brad Pitt and
10 Jennifer Aniston, who already look like brother and sister! When out and about, they
15 choose identical combats, sandals, jeans, black T-shirts, and even the same color
20 and style sunglasses. What is the message behind the dress-alike phenomenon°? Do couples who dress alike really believe that if they do everything together and in exactly the same way, their marriages or relationships will last
25 longer, or even forever? If so, they are going to have a terrible shock because, according to psychotherapists, the dress-alike phenomenon° is just a fad, and there is, at any rate, little hope for love which is based on dependency or a
30 notion° of perfect and permanent bliss.

One of the first—and initially shocking—messages from modern psychiatry is that the concept of romantic love is a myth. Even the notion of falling in love is problematic, as it has more to do with physical
35 attraction than with lasting love. In his book *The Road Less Traveled,* the famous psychiatrist and spiritual guru M. Scott Peck maintains that confusing physical attraction with love will always lead to misery. You may succeed in marrying the object of your desire, but you
40 will soon discover that what you thought was love was nothing more than an illusion°. Romance always fades, says Peck. With effort and discipline°, love might come later, but there is little connection between physical attraction and true love. True love is not dependency
45 either. If people's lives are ruled° or dictated by a relationship to the extent that they cannot do anything or go anywhere without their partners, they become depressed when faced with rejection° or separation.

True love finds a balance between togetherness and
50 separateness. Great marriages are those where partners enjoy time together as well as time apart. Genuine love respects each partner's individuality. Successful

marriages and partnerships are also those where both
partners adopt a healthy attitude to problems—all kinds of
55 problems. They accept that they are inevitable and work
together to resolve them. In this way they avoid the terrible
disillusionment that many couples experience when they
discover that there are things about their partners which
they do not like! Recent research has shown that some of
60 the most successful marriages and partnerships are LATs,
Live Apart Togethers. LATs are people who are married or
have a serious relationship but, for a variety of reasons, do
not live together permanently. They may work in different
parts of the country, for example. Many LATs eventually
65 move in together, having had time to experience and accept
each other's weaknesses, which makes a pleasant change
from moving out because they have only just discovered
them!

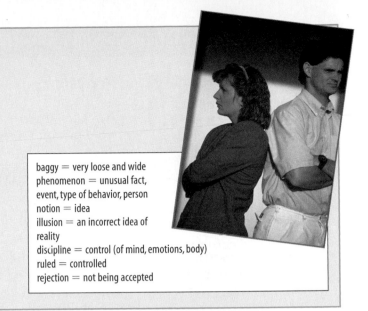

baggy = very loose and wide
phenomenon = unusual fact,
event, type of behavior, person
notion = idea
illusion = an incorrect idea of
reality
discipline = control (of mind, emotions, body)
ruled = controlled
rejection = not being accepted

4. an unusual but successful living arrangement
   for couples _____
5. the negative consequences of depending too
   much on a partner _____

3. Why do some people suffer from serious
   depression when they get divorced or
   separated?
4. Why do LATs have successful long-term
   relationships?

Second reading

C. Read the article again and find these facts.

1. What two things do these couples have in
   common: Madonna and her husband, Ronan
   Keating and his wife, and Brad Pitt and Jennifer
   Aniston?
2. What are Pitt's and Aniston's favorite casual
   clothes?
3. What do modern psychotherapists think of the
   dress-alike phenomenon?
4. According to Scott Peck, what things do people
   often confuse with true love?
5. How can couples change romantic love into
   true love?
6. What, according to Scott Peck, are some of the
   essential ingredients of a happy marriage?

Think about it

1. Are couples who follow the dress-alike fad
   more or less likely to stay together? Use
   information in the text to justify your answer.
2. Why does Scott Peck believe that romantic love
   is not an adequate basis for a happy marriage?

Vocabulary in context

D. Match the words and expressions from the text
in column 1 with the explanations or synonyms in
column 2.

Column 1

1. Line 8: clones
2. Line 29: bliss
3. Line 32: myth
4. Line 34: lasting
5. Line 36: guru
6. Line 37: misery
7. Line 44: dependency
8. Line 48: balance
9. Line 53: inevitable
10. Line 55: disillusionment

Column 2

a. complete happiness
b. an incorrect
   explanation of
   something
c. sure to happen
d. disappointment
e. exact copies
f. extreme unhappiness
g. a middle way
h. a leader or expert
i. permanent
j. constant need for
   someone else's
   company

Discussion

E. GROUP WORK Look again at the photos of
couples on the first page of this unit and use the
information in the reading text to discuss the
reasons why you think their relationships lasted or
didn't last.

Relative clauses: restrictive and nonrestrictive

Practice

A. Study these examples and notice what *who / that* refers to and the word or words it replaces.

1. Couples believe their marriages will last longer. They dress alike.
   Couples (who / that) dress alike believe that their marriages will last longer.
2. There is little hope for love. It is based on dependency.
   There is little hope for love (which / that) is based on dependency.
3. Those are the film stars. We saw them downtown last week.
   Those are the film stars (who/m / that) we saw downtown last week.
4. Romantic people later discover things about their partners. They do not like these things.
   Romantic people later discover things (which / that) they do not like about their partners.

B. Combine the following pairs of sentences with *who/m, that,* or *which.*

1. LATs are people. They are married but they do not live together.
2. Personally I don't believe all the suggestions. Scott Peck makes them.
3. Madonna and her husband were wearing clothes. They were the same color and style.
4. The dress-alike phenomenon is a fad. I think it's crazy.
5. I know a lot of people. They have gotten divorced and still remained friends.
6. Nicole Kidman is the film star. I admire her most.

C. Underline the nonrestrictive clauses in the following sentences.

1. Jimmy Carter, who still helps developing countries, was U.S. president from 1977-1981.
2. Seoul, which is one of my favorite Asian cities, is situated on the River Han.
3. The U.S. Open, which most tennis stars would love to win, is a tennis tournament.
4. Zinedine Zidane, whom I would love to meet, is a French soccer player.

D. Combine these pairs of sentences. Don't forget the commas.

1. *The Road Less Traveled* is easy to read. Scott Peck wrote it.
2. Some of Peck's ideas are very unusual. His ideas make me think a lot.
3. Sigmund Freud was the father of modern psychotherapy. He was born in Austria.
4. Freud's techniques became very popular at the end of the 19th century. People still use his techniques today.
5. My brother and his wife have a life-apart-together lifestyle. I admire them very much.

Relative clauses: restrictive and nonrestrictive

Meaning	Example	Rules / Guidelines
Restrictive clauses		
The information in the clause provides essential information. Without this information, the sentence may lose its meaning or the meaning may change or be incomplete.	LATs are people who live apart but have a permanent relationship.	The relative *that* can replace *who* or *which* in these clauses. It is incorrect to use commas. You can omit the relative pronoun, if it is the object of the clause.
Nonrestrictive clauses		
The clause contains additional information that is not essential to the meaning.	Zinedine Zidane, who/m I would love to meet, is an incredible soccer player.	Use *who/m* and *which* only. Always use commas. Never omit the relative pronoun.

Test yourself

E. Complete the text with *who/m, that,* or *which,* adding commas if necessary.

Today, life is becoming very difficult for young couples **(1)** _____ work. Many of them would like to have children **(2)** _____ would bring joy into their lives, but their working conditions **(3)** _____ often consist of long hours and low salaries, make it impossible for them to have children. Some couples are luckier than others. They work in companies **(4)** _____ understand their problems and help them by offering special care for small children in the workplace. In this way, employees **(5)** _____ have children but can't afford to give up their jobs can visit their babies during breaks. This arrangement **(6)** _____ is still very rare in most parts of the world, is an ideal solution to the problem of couples **(7)** _____ want to have children but **(8)** _____ can't afford to stop working.

Asking for and giving reasons

Why is that? Can you explain why ... ? How come ... ?

One reason for this is ... That's because ... For one thing, ... Another reason is ...

Think about it

A. Think about the answers to these questions.

What personal qualities are important for a good relationship with a spouse, partner, or close friend? Why are they important? Take notes.

EXAMPLE: *kindness, a good sense of humor*

B. PAIR WORK Share your ideas with your partner and explain your reasons. Use some of the expressions from the box above.

C. GROUP WORK Together, choose ONE quality that you all think is important for a happy relationship. Work together to plan a short oral report, explaining your answer and giving reasons and examples. All group members should take notes.

D. GROUP WORK Form a new group with students who prepared different reports. Take turns giving reports to your group. While you listen to the other students, take notes on the qualities listed and the reasons given.

Important quality	Reasons
1. _____	_____
2. _____	_____
3. _____	_____
4. _____	_____
5. _____	_____

E. Discuss the reports you heard. Did class members have similar or different ideas? Were there any surprising ideas?

A recent survey asked the question, "Are married people happier than single people?" In the United States, 53% said yes, while 47% of British and only 34% of Australians said yes.

A. Read the text and try to determine the meanings of the three-word verbs. Choose the meanings of the three-word verbs from the box and write their meanings in the chart.

understand	finish or complete	accept	experience or have
tolerate or accept	leave or abandon	find or propose	

Most couples **come up against** serious problems in their relationships. Some people cope with these problems very badly. They do not try to **come up with** a solution. Instead, they simply **walk out on** their partners, because they feel that they cannot **put up with** them anymore. This is shocking behavior and almost always leads to the end of the relationship. Others adopt a more mature attitude. They **face up to** their problems together, discuss them, and try to resolve them. These couples are more likely to have lasting relationships or to **get along with** one another even if they **go through with** a divorce.

Three-word verb	Meaning
1. to come up against (a problem, a difficulty, an obstacle)	experience / have
2. to come up with (a solution, an idea, a plan)	_____
3. to walk out on (a partner, an employer)	_____
4. to put up with (a person, people, a situation, behavior you don't like)	_____
5. to face up to (a difficult situation, a problem)	_____
6. to get along with (a person, people)	_____
7. to go through with (a difficult process e.g. a divorce, a wedding ceremony, a dangerous plan)	_____

B. Use the three-word verbs above to complete the text.

1. I'm so busy these days. Our secretary _____ us last week, so I have to do all the secretarial work myself.

2. He is often rather bad-tempered. I tell you, he's not the easiest guy _____.

3. Listen, we simply must _____ it. We don't have enough money to go on vacation this year, so let's forget about making plans.

4. He couldn't _____ the long hours in his last job, so he resigned.

5. That company had serious financial problems, but fortunately the director _____ some good ideas for solving them.

Paying attention to sequence words

Listen for sequence words to help you understand the events in a story. When talking about events, speakers show the order that things happen by using sequence words like

first	in the beginning	at first
later	after that	next
finally	in the end	at last

Before you listen

A. PAIR WORK You are going to listen to the story of a woman who was happily married for many years. Talk about these questions with your partner.

1. Do you know anyone who has been married for a very long time, for example, your grandparents or other relatives? How long have they been married?

2. How did this couple meet and get married? Tell what you know using some of the sequence words listed above.

3. Has this couple ever given you advice about relationships? If so, what did they say?

First listening

B. Bridget Moen is ninety-two years old and has had two very happy marriages. Listen and write down two pieces of advice she gives about marriage.

1. _____

2. _____

Second listening

C. Listen again and write numbers to put the events in the correct order.

_____ She met Everett.

_____ Walter went to thirteen parties at the dancing school.

_____ She met Walter.

_____ Everett invited her to a restaurant for lunch.

_____ Her first husband died.

_____ She and Walter got married.

_____ Walter started a barber shop.

_____ Everett gave her flowers.

_____ She and Everett got married.

After listening

D. PAIR WORK What is your opinion of Bridget's advice? What do you think is important for a good marriage?

Test yourself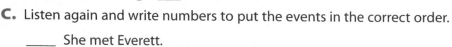

E. You hear two friends discussing a lecture about the stages of marriage. Which is the last stage?

1. Acceptance   2. You're perfect   3. Transformation

Writing a letter giving advice

Before you write

A. GROUP WORK Discuss the questions. Would you ever write to a magazine or newspaper for advice? Why or why not? Now, look at these letters. What is Christine's problem? What does Steve suggest? What do you think of his suggestion?

Dear Readers,

I'm writing about my aunt. Maybe you can give me some advice. (She would never write to a magazine like this herself!) She is 45 years old and single. She has a wonderful job and a great lifestyle. She works hard, but she also has a number of hobbies. **For example,** she sings in a folk group and she goes bowling once a week. **In addition,** she has lots of really good friends, whom she sees all the time. **However,** sometimes I think she worries about her future, especially about getting old. She wonders if she'll feel lonely when she's not so active. **Also,** I think she sometimes wishes she had someone to share her life with. She was married once, a long time ago. Maybe she should try looking for a partner again. What do you think?

Christine

Replies from readers

Dear Christine,

My mom was in a similar situation to you a few years ago when my dad died. I think your aunt is very wise to face up to the fact that she might feel lonely in old age. **However,** in the case of my mom, she thought that a second marriage wasn't really right for her. **Instead,** when I left home to get married, she decided to rent out my old room on a regular basis to an overseas student. And you cannot imagine how much she has benefited from this arrangement. She tells me she learns so much from the students. She says that now she has "sons" and "daughters" from all over the world, all of whom have promised to send their sons and daughters to look after her in her old age!

Steve

Dear Christine,

My dad is in a similar situation to yours. He's single (my parents divorced twelve years ago), he's fifty, he has a wonderful job, great friends. But looking at his position, I do not think a second marriage is a good idea.

In fact, it could cause you a lot of problems. **For example,** _____

Instead, I think you should

_____

_____

_____

In addition, / Also you could

_____ **However,**

you must remember that

_____

Marie

Write

B. PAIR WORK Look carefully at how _however, instead, for example, in addition,_ and _also_ are used in the letters in A. Work in pairs and complete this letter that Marie wrote to Christine.

8 Putting It Together

Happy Couples	Unhappy Couples
Do things together but also have separate interests	Never face up to problems

A. PAIR WORK Imagine you and your partner are a couple. Decide whether you are going to be a happy or an unhappy couple. Then write a list of at least five reasons why you are a happy or an unhappy couple.

B. GROUP WORK Now work with another pair of students. Do not tell them whether you are a happy or an unhappy couple. Take turns asking one another about your relationship. After you have asked at least five questions, decide whether you think the other couple is happy or unhappy and the reasons for your decisions.

C. Work alone and think of a happy or unhappy couple whom you know or have known and who stayed together for most of their lives. Write notes about the reasons why they stayed together and why they were happy, or why they stayed together and were unhappy. Use the notes to describe the couple to the class.

Stayed together and were happy
Did not build their relationship on romantic love alone
Tolerant of each other's individuality

Stayed together and were unhappy
Could not put up with one another's weaknesses
Worried about what people would say if they went through with a divorce

D. CLASS TASK With the class, discuss the following topic:
Marriages were happier and better twenty years ago than they are today.

For more about couples, view the CNN video. Activities to accompany the video begin on page 137.

1 Warm Up

Music

A. Look at the pictures. Do you recognize any of these bands or performers? What type of music do they play?

Reuters NewMedia Inc./CORBIS

Reuters NewMedia Inc./CORBIS

CORBIS

CORBIS

Communication
Talking about music

Discussing tastes in cultural activities

Asking about likes and dislikes

Grammar
Reviewing uses of present perfect and simple past

Contrasting present perfect with simple past

Vocabulary
Musical groups and instruments

Money problems and solutions

Skills
Reading an expository text: feature article

Listening and predicting vocabulary

Writing an informal letter

B. PAIR WORK Discuss the words in the box and match them to the appropriate headings.

Types of music	Musical instruments	Types of musical groupings

C. GROUP WORK Use the words from the box to make sentences about music you like.

EXAMPLE: *Metallica is my favorite rock band.*

rock jazz guitar band piano organ pop reggae choir orchestra folk opera hip-hop quartet classical trio

Acquiring new vocabulary as you read

Analyze words by looking at prefixes and suffixes. Identify the function of the word, for example, noun, verb, or adjective.

Before you read

A. PAIR WORK What kind of music do you think this group sings?

First reading

B. Skim the text and decide which paragraph contains the description.

1. the changes the Vienna Boys' Choir has made over the past few years _____
2. the traditions of the Vienna Boys' Choir _____
3. the origins and history of the choir _____
4. the reasons why the choir has had to make certain changes _____

Change or Die

One of the oldest musical institutions in the world, the Vienna Boys' Choir, was established in 1498 by Emperor Maximilian I. Its brief° was to sing exclusively for the court° in church services, at private concerts, and
5 on state occasions. For the next 400 years, that is exactly what it did, receiving at the same time full financial support from the state. When the Hapsburg Empire disintegrated in 1918, however, the choir became an independent institution and soon learned to stand on its
10 own two feet. The Austrian state continues, even today, to provide some support for the institution in the form of rent-free accommodation in the Augartenpalais, a government-owned palace in a park in the center of Vienna, but this represents a very tiny contribution to the
15 enormous budget the choir needs for its survival.

Superficially, the Vienna Boys' Choir has not changed over the past 500 years. The boys still wear sailor suits—navy blue for daytime performances and cream for evening wear.
20 Their repertoire is still mostly religious and classical music, with Mozart, Haydn, and Schubert as their favorite
25 sources. They still work very hard, practicing for two and a half hours every afternoon, after completing a normal day at school. What's more,
30 they give an average of about 300 public performances a year, of which at least 200 are abroad. In 2000, for

35 example, they gave a staggering 342 performances, 209 of which were abroad—a tougher schedule than
40 any ever undertaken by even the most resilient° of rock bands, such as the Rolling Stones.

A closer look at the
45 activities of the choir reveals, however, that times have changed. With the steep rise in the cost of living in Austria in the latter part of the 20th century, the
50 choir ran into serious financial difficulties and, at one point, the future of one of Europe's oldest cultural institutions looked very bleak indeed. One solution to the
55 financial predicament was to organize even more performances, as the money collected from the sale of tickets represents a major source° of income for the choir.
60 This option was out of the question, however, as the boys are very young— aged nine to fourteen— and they already have a grueling academic and
65 musical schedule.

In the end, diversification° into other types of music was the solution to the problem. As
70 a result, the Vienna Boys'

Choir has, over the past few years, established partnerships with popular singers such as Freddie Mercury, Coolio, and Whitney Houston. It has also provided soundtracks for a Japanese animated movie and
75 for films such as *Primal Fear* and *The 13th Floor*. The boys have even produced a boy band act complete with hip-hop routine for the Alpine Skiing World Cup and have brought out a new version of Celine Dion's title song from *Titanic*. They have gotten into music with an international
80 flavor, too, and have performed in a show called *Inspiration*, 30 minutes of spiritual music and percussion° from Africa, India, Pakistan, and Israel. But, perhaps most adventurous of all, they have produced an album of cover

versions of popular songs by rock groups like Metallica.
85 Thus, the Vienna Boys' Choir is no longer the old-fashioned institution people believed it to be, but a lively, modern group of singers with a youthful and international appeal—in short, the Vienna Boys' Choir is now one of the best boy bands in the world!

---

brief = official instructions to do something (formal word)
the court = place where kings, queens, or emperors live
resilient = able to recover one's strength quickly
source = place something comes from
diversification = increase in the variety of activities
percussion = musical instruments such as drums, cymbals, and tambourines

---

Second reading

C. Find these facts.

1. Where did the choir work during its first 400 years?

2. Where did it get its money from during this time?

3. What kind of support does the Austrian government give the choir today?

4. What kinds of music has the choir started to sing recently?

Think about it

1. Why was the state unable to give support to the choir after 1918?

2. Why didn't the choir solve its financial problems by giving more performances?

3. How has the choir tried to solve its financial problems?

4. Why do you think the author says it was adventurous of the choir to sing versions of songs by Metallica?

Vocabulary in context

D. Read the text again and choose the most suitable meaning for the words as they are used in the reading.

1. Line 8: disintegrated
   a. came to an end   c. changed direction
   b. moved to another place

2. Line 9: stand on its own feet
   a. avoid falling   c. recover from a
   b. be independent   problem

3. Line 16: superficially
   a. on the surface   c. in the end
   b. in general

4. Line 47: steep
   a. quite gradual   c. very big
   b. rather unexpected

5. Line 50: ran into
   a. crashed with   c. moved quickly
   b. experienced

6. Line 54: bleak
   a. cold   c. hopeless
   b. unpredictable

7. Line 55: predicament
   a. difficulty   c. illness
   b. challenge

8. Line 60: out of the question
   a. not a possibility   c. a weak alternative
   b. an unlikely choice

9. Line 64: grueling
   a. extremely hard   c. unbelievably varied
   b. really fascinating

10. Line 71: established partnerships
    a. worked together   c. organized a business
       with   with
    b. got married to

Discussion

E. GROUP WORK Discuss the choice of the title *Change or Die* for this reading. Think of all the reasons why the author chose this title. Do you like the title? Why or why not? If you do not like it, suggest a different title and justify your choice.

Uses of the present perfect

Practice

A. Complete the text with the correct form and tense of the verb.

have	complain	continue
be	deteriorate	travel.

Although most parents whose sons are members of the Vienna Boys' Choir are happy with their children's education, last year, some **(1)** _____ because they believe the boys work too hard. Over the past months, for example, the boys **(2)** _____ to many different countries and, at the same time, they **(3)** _____ to do their normal academic work. The living conditions of the boys in Vienna are not ideal either. The inside of the Augartenpalais, where the choir has been resident for some time, **(4)** _____ a lot. The choir **(5)** _____ financial difficulties in the last decade of the 20th century, so it has been unable to maintain the building. Consequently, the boys' rooms are rather cold and unwelcoming. Despite these disadvantages, most boys enjoy their lives as choristers within a musical institution that for centuries **(6)** _____ one of the most respected in Europe.

B. Fill in the blanks with the correct tense and form of the verb.

make	hear	(just) buy
record	change.	

1. I _____ an incredible CD. Do you want to hear it?
2. My taste in music _____ a lot over the past few years.
3. Pavarotti _____ recordings with singers like Sting and Tina Turner.
4. Last year one of my friends _____ his first album.
5. _____ the latest release by Santana yet? I think it's great.

C. Complete the text with the correct tense and form of the verb.

hear	(never) like	
(not) stop	(always) enjoy	
be	decide.	

I **(1)** *have always enjoyed* rock music but I **(2)** _____ classical music. Then, last week, when I **(3)** _____ in Los Angeles, I **(4)** _____ some music by Bond. Do you know about them? They are beautiful women who play classical music in a very different style. I was so impressed that I **(5)** _____ to buy their CD. I **(6)** _____ listening to it since I got back.

FYI

The definite article *the* is used with things— institutions, buildings, ships, people—that are unique, i.e., of which there is only one.

D. PAIR WORK Find examples in the text about the Vienna Boys' Choir in which the definite article *the* is used with:

1. the name of an empire _____
2. the name of a building _____
3. the name of a famous rock band _____
4. the name of a sporting event _____

E. Write the definite article where you need it in the sentences opposite. Write *X* where you do not need it and discuss with your partner the reasons for your decisions.

1. Many people on the Greek islands live in _____ white houses.
2. _____ President of the United States lives in _____ White House.
3. I love _____ opera. It is my favorite kind of music.
4. _____ Paris Opera is a beautiful historical building in central Paris.
5. At the zoo you can see _____ monkeys, bears, and lions.
6. _____ Doors were a famous rock group in the '60s.

Home work

Uses of the present perfect

Examples	Use
1. The Vienna Boys' Choir has been performing since 1498.	To talk about an action or situation that began in the past and is still true in the present
2. Times have changed for the Vienna Boys' Choir.	To talk about actions or events that have finished but are still recent, or are recent news
3. The choir has just finished singing.	To talk about something that happened in the immediate past
4. The Vienna Boys' Choir has traveled a lot.	To talk about actions and events that are part of our experience
5. (a) The Choir has already established partnerships with famous pop singers. (b) So far, they have recorded the soundtracks for two films. (c) They haven't won any pop awards yet.	With expressions like *already, yet, so far* (a) to emphasize how quickly or slowly things have been done (b) and (c) to report progress up to the present point in ongoing or repeated actions

Present vs. the simple past

Present perfect	Simple past
I've just finished.	*I finished recording my new record last week.*
I've finished already.	*Paul left the studio a couple of minutes ago.*
To talk about an action or state that has stopped in the recent past, or to comment on progress in a schedule with no specific time reference.	To talk about an action or state that stopped at a specific point of time in the past—even the recent past.
Have you ever lived in Los Angeles?	*Did you live in Los Angeles for many years?*
I've had two cups of tea today.	
To relate past actions or states to present experience; these actions may happen again	To refer to actions or states that continued for a long time in the past but no longer happen or are no longer true.
I've been to Central Park several times.	*When I was a child in New York, my parents took me to Central Park every Sunday.*
To talk about repeated past actions that have happened up to the present time. They have no specific past time reference and could happen again.	To talk about actions or habits that were repeated in the past but that are no longer true or no longer happen.

Test yourself

F. Match the uses on the right with the examples on the left.

1. That singer has just recorded a new album.
2. I saw the Beatles when I was a kid.
3. Did the audience enjoy the performance?
4. Have you practiced the piano today?
5. We went to a concert every Sunday.
6. They've released two new CDs so far this year.
7. Did you see Coolio on TV last night?
8. Has the choir started its performance yet?

a. check progress in a schedule or plan
b. actions completed in the past (3 examples)
c. recent past actions, no specific time
d. repeated past actions that could happen again within same time period (2 examples)
e. actions repeated and completed in the past

Home work

Think about it

Speaking focus

Asking about likes and dislikes

Here are some ways to ask questions:
Who is your favorite …?
Do you like … ? Is there any … you dislike? What kind of … do you like?

A. PAIR WORK Ask your partner questions about the topics below. Make notes about your partner's answers.

any instruments you are able to play

favorite kinds of music, and why

any kind of music you dislike, and why

favorite musicians or groups, and why

concerts attended

B. GROUP WORK Join another pair. Introduce your partner to the others and tell them about your partner's tastes in music.

C. GROUP WORK You and your group are the directors of a charity called People for a Better World, and you are planning a benefit concert to raise money for your organization. You want to attract a big audience to the concert, and you also want to record a live album of the concert to earn more money. Choose three famous musicians or bands to perform at your concert. Then choose two songs that you will ask each one to perform.

Band or Musician	Songs	
1. _____	A. _____	B. _____
2. _____	A. _____	B. _____
3. _____	A. _____	B. _____

D. Now share your group's plans with the class, and explain why you chose these musicians and these songs.

Many famous musicians have played at benefit concerts to raise money for charity. At a benefit concert, groups and musicians donate their work, and the money from ticket sales and albums goes to charity organizations. The first benefit concert was the Concert for Bangladesh in 1971, organized by ex-Beatle George Harrison, which collected millions of dollars to fight poverty in that country. Since then, many other benefit concerts have raised money to help refugees, people in need, and victims of disasters.

5 Vocabulary in Detail

the soundtrack   a release   a title song   a show   a repertoire   a performance

FYI A definition explains the meaning and the use of a word or an expression.

A. Here are some of the music-related words from this unit. Match the words with the definitions.

1. This is the word for all the pieces of music a person or group knows well. It can also be used for the plays and operas theater groups and opera companies perform. *a repertoire*

2. This is the word for a record that has just come out. It can also be used with videos. *a release*

3. This is an informal word for a musical event. It can also be used for variety programs. *a show*

4. This refers to the music that you hear during a movie, but it is also used to refer to the combination of music, speech, and other sounds in a movie. *The soundtrack*

5. This is a formal word for the singing or playing of a piece of music by an individual or a group. It can also be used with dancing and the theater (plays). *a performance*

6. The main piece of music in a movie. *title song*

B. Complete the text with one of the words from A.

1. What a terrible movie! The *title song* was awful. I couldn't hear a word the actors were saying.

2. Let's go to a *show* on the weekend—something relaxing and entertaining. How about a jazz concert?

3. I've just been to the opera. What an amazing *repertoire*!

4. Few bands have ever had as impressive a *performance* as the Beatles. I've lost count of how many albums they recorded.

5. Can you call the video store and check what new _____ they have this week?

6. What's that music? Isn't it the _____ from *Moulin Rouge?*

FYI Synonyms or synonymous expressions have the same or a similar meaning to another word or expression in a given context.

C. Match the words and expressions about money on the left with the synonyms or synonymous expressions on the right.

1. financial support   **a.** got into debt

2. stand on your own two feet **b.** earnings

3. a rise in the cost of living **c.** an increase in everyday expenses

4. ran into serious financial difficulties **d.** funding

5. source of income   **e.** pay your own way

Listening strategy

Predicting vocabulary

Before you listen, think about the topic and try to guess some of the words you will hear. This will help you to understand what you hear better.

Before you listen

A. PAIR WORK You are going to listen to a talk on the history of the guitar. With a partner, list six words that you think you might hear.

First listening

B. Listen to the talk and circle the words from your list that you heard.

C. PAIR WORK Compare your answers with your partner. If you're not sure about a word, look it up in a dictionary or check with your teacher.

Second listening

D. Listen again and complete the chart.

E. PAIR WORK Compare your answers with your partner's and add any

Time	Place	Event
_____	Babylonia	_____
_____	_____	____first written mention of the guitar _____
16th cent.	_____	_____guitar with seven _____
_____	Spain	___Fernando Sor's book _____
19th cent.	South America	_____
1936	_____	_____
_____	_____	___amplifier and electric guitar with solid body _____

information that you missed.

After listening

F. GROUP WORK According to the talk, why is the guitar so popular now? Do you like to listen to guitar music? How many members of your group can play the guitar?

Test yourself

G. You are going to listen to a radio announcement about a concert. Look at the questions, and think about words you might hear in the announcement. Then listen and answer.

1. How much do the tickets cost?
   a. $8   b. $9   c. $12   d. $20
2. How can you buy tickets?
   a. in the mail   b. by phone   c. at the theater   d. from a web site
3. Which of these things will you NOT hear at the concert?
   a. singing   b. guitar music   c. jazz   d. an orchestra

7 Writing

An informal letter

Before you write

A. In some tests of writing, you are asked to write an informal letter to a friend. It is important to organize your letter carefully. It is a good idea to underline the details that are asked for in the question. It is important to include all the details that are asked for. It is also important to divide your letter into paragraphs and include a greeting and a closing. It is important to read directions carefully. Look at the directions below and underline the details that are asked for.

Paragraph 1: Greeting →

Paragraph 2: Comment on personal information from letter received. Invent this information in your letter. →

Paragraph 3: Introduce the main topic. →

Paragraph 4: Describe the main topic in more detail. →

Paragraph 5: Closing →

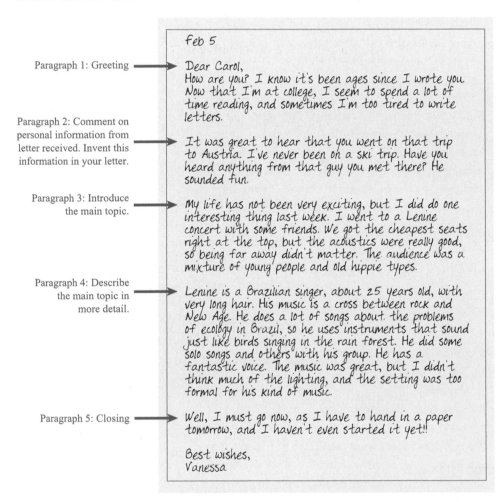

Feb 5

Dear Carol,
How are you? I know it's been ages since I wrote you. Now that I'm at college, I seem to spend a lot of time reading, and sometimes I'm too tired to write letters.

It was great to hear that you went on that trip to Austria. I've never been on a ski trip. Have you heard anything from that guy you met there? He sounded fun.

My life has not been very exciting, but I did do one interesting thing last week. I went to a Lenine concert with some friends. We got the cheapest seats right at the top, but the acoustics were really good, so being far away didn't matter. The audience was a mixture of young people and old hippie types.

Lenine is a Brazilian singer, about 25 years old, with very long hair. His music is a cross between rock and New Age. He does a lot of songs about the problems of ecology in Brazil, so he uses instruments that sound just like birds singing in the rain forest. He did some solo songs and others with his group. He has a fantastic voice. The music was great, but I didn't think much of the lighting, and the setting was too formal for his kind of music.

Well, I must go now, as I have to hand in a paper tomorrow, and I haven't even started it yet!!

Best wishes,
Vanessa

Write

Last week you had the opportunity to go to a concert of your favorite musical group. Write a letter to a friend, describing the concert. Include details such as the way the performers and audience were dressed, the kind of music you heard and the special effects you saw and give reasons why you enjoyed or disliked the concert. Write approximately 150 words. Do not forget to make your writing look like a letter.

Role play

Read the description of the situation and the school in the role play below. Choose your roles. Work alone for five minutes. Read your role cards carefully and prepare arguments to support your point of view. Make some notes of your ideas. Then act out the role play.

Situation: A 16-year-old student who is extremely talented musically has won a place at a performing arts school where he or she will be able to develop his or her musical talents as a pianist. *The school* is free, is located in a big city on the other side of the country, and has wonderful teachers. The living conditions for students are very basic: the schedule is grueling because, in addition to studying music and normal high school classes, students travel a lot. Some of the students who graduate from this school go on to become famous musicians or singers. However, some suffer serious emotional problems. A large number have a wonderful time while they are there, but they do not pursue a musical career after they leave school.

Role 1:
The student is sensitive, a little shy, and very close to his or her best friend and younger brother or sister. Apart from his or her formal piano studies, the student also plays the keyboard in a rock band with some friends. The band is starting to become well known locally. However, the student loves classical piano and wants to go to the special school.

Role 2:
The younger brother or sister has always been close to the student and would miss him or her terribly if he or she were to leave. The younger sibling does not have any special talent for music and does not play any instrument. The younger sibling has no real friends of his or her own and depends a lot on the older brother or sister.

Role 3:
The singer from the student's band has high hopes for the band and wants them to stay together. He or she and the student were the first to form the band and have always been loyal to each other. In recent months they have started writing songs together. He or she admires the student's ability as a classical pianist but doesn't like that type of music.

For more about music, view the CNN video. Activities to accompany the video begin on page 138.

Role 4:
The student's best friend is very happy living where he or she lives and can't see why anyone would want to leave. He or she has heard frightening stories about life in the big city and about performing arts schools where the students feel "burned out" before they even finish their studies.

Review Your Grammar

A. Complete the sentences with the past tense, the present perfect tense, or the –ing form of the verb.

1. (know)   Jerry _has known_ Linda for about six months.
2. (meet)   He _met_ her at a party at his cousin Bill's house.
3. (have)   They _having_ a mutual interest in sports, they got along well.
4. (agree)   Linda immediately _agreed_ to go out with Jerry.
5. (not tell) They _haven't told_ Bill yet, but they will soon.
6. (listen)   Linda and Jerry enjoy _listening_ to music.
7. (see)   They _saw_ Bill at a concert last week.
8. (leave)   They _left_ quickly so that he wouldn't see them.

B. Circle the word or words that correctly completes each sentence.

1. I just saw a movie (who / whom / (that) / which) I loved.
2. Have you ever (see / saw / (seen)) *Time Trackers?*
3. It's about a woman (who / whom / (that) / which) invents a time machine.
4. She looks forward to (travel / will travel / (traveling)) into the future.
5. However, she hasn't (practice / (practiced) / practicing) enough.
6. She has trouble (set / to set / (setting)) the dials and ends up in the year 800.

High Challenge

C. Rewrite each sentence so that it says the same thing in a different way. Use the words in parentheses.

EXAMPLE:
    My brother does not enjoy going shopping. (dislike)
    My brother dislikes going shopping.

1. Jason has eaten breakfast already. (just)
Jason has just eaten breakfast already
2. Fashion slaves are people. They feel they have to be well dressed at all times. (who)
Fashion slaves are people, who feel they have to be well dressed
3. Some people never buy clothes. (avoid)
Some people avoid buy clothes
4. They don't like to spend hours at the mall. (don't look forward to)
They don't look forward to spending hours at the mall
5. Do you ever spend all day at the mall? (spent)
Do you ever

FOR Sale

FYI

Exercises asking you to rewrite sentences using new words and structures are often found on international examinations. It is important to look at the original sentence carefully before rewriting to make sure that you include the main idea and all the details in the rewritten sentence.

Review Your Vocabulary

A. Use words from the box to complete the conversation.

> inevitable   income   bleak   misery   friends   predicament   fashionable
> source   question   made

Mario: I'm in a real **(1)** _____!

Tom: Well what's the **(2)** _____ of your problem?

Mario: I'm invited to a fancy wedding and I have to wear something **(3)** _____.

Tom: It was **(4)** _inevitable_ that you'd have to buy some new clothes some-day.

Mario: But I just quit my job and I don't have any source of **(5)** _income_.

Tom: Well, the outlook isn't totally **(6)** _bleak_.

Mario: What do you mean? I'm in **(7)** _misery_.

Tom: My brother has a lot of well **(8)** _made_ clothes. You're about his size.

Mario: Thanks, but I couldn't do that. It's out of the **(9)** _question_. I don't know him.

Tom: Don't be silly! You don't have to be **(10)** _friends_ with him to bor-row his clothes. I do it all the time!

B. Complete each sentence by putting the words in parentheses in the correct order.

1. (have, relationship, had, a)
   Lesley and Arturo _have had a relationship_ for several years.

2. (to, attracted, him, was)
   She _was attracted to him_ because of his intelligence.

3. (her, feet, on, own, two, stand)
   Arturo likes Lesley because she can _stand up on her own_

4. (with, up, come)
   Arturo wants to ask Lesley to marry him, but he can't
   Come up with the right words.

5. (him, out, on, walk)
   If Arturo doesn't ask soon, Lesley may _walk out on_. him

6. (up, break, him, with)
   However, she really doesn't want to _break up with him_.

C. Circle the word in each group that doesn't belong.

1. casual   (scruffy)   overdressed   useful
2. pop   (drab)   folk   opera
3. divorced   separated   (engaged)   (balanced)
4. baggy   well made   (steep)   beautifully finished
5. (happiness)   rejection   misery   disillusionment
6. survive   put up with   face up to   (quit)

Review Your Speaking

Fluency

A. PAIR WORK Look at this photo and describe it to your partner. Then ask your partner the questions.

How do you think the couple met?
Why were they attracted to each other?
Do you think their marriage will survive?

B. GROUP WORK Work in groups of three. Choose one of the roles below and try to reach an agreement.

1. You are a wedding planner. The couple who are going to get married have very different ideas about what the wedding should be like. Try to help them reach an agreement.
2. You are the groom. You would like to have a big wedding with live music and all your friends and family invited, but you do not feel it is necessary to provide an elaborate meal.
3. You are the bride. Your family enjoys eating in expensive restaurants, but you know they will expect a good meal at your wedding. You would prefer a small wedding with excellent food.

F•A•Q

Frequently Ask Questions

I know I make mistakes when I speak or write in English, but I can't see my own mistakes. How can I learn to notice mistakes?

When you are speaking English, you are so busy thinking about what you want to say that it is difficult to monitor your speech. If you are not sure whether you are making mistakes or not, try tape recording some of your conversations and listen to them later to check if you can hear mistakes. You should not worry too much about slips, but notice if you make the same mistake over and over again.

It is easier to check for mistakes in writing. It is a good idea to write something and then leave it for a few hours before you go back and read it again; sometimes we can not see our own mistakes immediately after we write. It is also a good idea to have somebody else look over your writing; exchanging writing with another student can be helpful. Another option is to find someone who is more advanced in English to check your writing.

Review Your Listening

Listening 1 🎧

A. You are going to listen to an interview with a violinist. Write some words you think you might hear.

_____   _____   _____   _____   _____

_____   _____   _____   _____   _____

B. Listen and circle the words you did hear.

C. Listen again and fill in the answers.

- Name _____
- Started playing the violin _____
- Education _____
- Now plays in a group with _____
- Where they play _____
- Kind of music they play _____

Listening 2 🎧

D. Now you'll hear an interview with Mark, the violinist's husband. He plays modern electronic music. What do you think Sally's opinion is about that kind of music? Do you think they have any problems?

_____

_____

E. Listen and check your guesses.

F. Listen again and fill in the answers.

- Married for _____
- Other instruments played _____, _____, _____
- Made an album with _____
- Started writing music with _____
- Sally's opinion: 1) _____
- 2) _____
- Mark's advice _____

1 Warm Up

Soccer

A. Work with a partner and describe the mascots in the pictures.

- What are the mascots wearing?
- What colors are their clothes?
- Which countries do you think they represent?

- Why do you think each country has this mascot?
- Which year do you think these were the mascots for the soccer World Cup?

Communication

Talking about sports

Agreeing and disagreeing

Describing and justifying choices in detail

Grammar

Past perfect

Past perfect contrasted with simple past

Vocabulary

Sports and sporting events

Soccer and styles of playing

Noun + gerund as compound adjective

Skills

Reading for inference and detail: encyclopedia excerpt

Listening and making inferences

Writing: justifying choices

B. Work with a partner and check (✓) the headings which apply to each of the sports in the column on the left. Put (X) if they do not apply.

Sport/Type	Team	Individual	Outside	Inside	Winter	Summer
Soccer						
Golf						
Skiing						
Basketball						
Ice hockey						
Wind surfing						
Tennis						

C. Talk about the sports in the chart.

EXAMPLE: *Soccer is a team sport. We usually play it outside in cold or cool weather, but we can also play in hot weather—on the beach, for example.*

Reading strategy

Skimming for the general idea

Before you read a text in detail, skim through it to get a general idea of the topic.

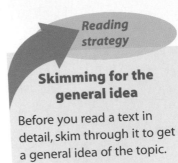

Before you read

A. PAIR WORK How popular is soccer in your country? What are the names of the most important teams? What sort of mascots do famous teams have? Which other sports are important in your country? Which sports do you watch and which do you play?

First reading

B. Skim the text and choose a suitable title for the article from the list.

1. Women in Soccer History
2. Historical Changes to Soccer Rules
3. Making Soccer History

Although the distant origins of soccer can be traced back thousands of years, the modern game is a **dynamic** sport, often undergoing significant changes in its rules, its players, its team formations, and in the
5 organization of its important events. In the 1950s, the Brazilian national team, with its innovative team strategies, changed the way the game is played. Japan and Korea found a new way to organize soccer's greatest tournament, offering shared venues° for the World Cup in
10 2002. But soccer is not just a man's game. In many parts of the world women have **struggled,** with varying degrees of success°, to achieve recognition for women's soccer. Recent years have seen them make great advances.

In 1958, Brazil won the World Cup in Sweden. This
15 was a surprise win for two reasons. First, because no other Latin American team before had ever won when the finals took place outside Latin America. And secondly, because Brazil had never won the Cup before. Their **victory** was unforgettable, not just because of their
20 skill, speed, and goal-scoring ability but also because they caught their opponents off guard° by changing the traditional 5-3-2 team formation. Brazil's new approach permitted° much greater **flexibility.** When defending, they used the 4-3-3 formation with four players
25 defending at the back, three in midfield, and three in the attack. While **attacking,** they **reversed** the formation and placed four men up front. From then onwards, soccer changed forever, with teams all over the world taking their cue° from the **flamboyant** Brazilians and
30 experimenting with a greater variety of formations.

While Brazil influenced the way soccer is played on the field, Japan and Korea completely changed the way soccer's World Cup is organized. They became the first Asian nations ever to **host** the finals and the first
35 countries to do this together. Until 2002, the World Cup

had taken place in only one country each time, but Japan and Korea formed a partnership°, using a total of twenty stadiums, ten in Japan and ten in Korea, to meet the needs of the thousands of soccer fans that **flocked**
40 to Asia from all over the world. Most of the stadiums were new and designed to the highest standards, so this also contributed to making the 2002 World Cup very memorable for the fans.

The time when a
45 women's World Cup attracts the same interest and excitement as the men's event is probably still a long way off, but
50 historically speaking, women's role in the story of soccer starts a surprisingly long time ago. The first known
55 **records** of women's soccer are some Chinese frescoes of women playing soccer at the time of the
60 Donghan Dynasty° (A.D. 25-220). Women's soccer then

seems to have disappeared with the next dynasty, the
Quings. In the late 19th century, records show that
women's soccer matches were very popular in Scotland,
65 where married women played against single women. In
the 20th century, however, the women's game was
banned° in England, Holland, and Germany. Then, in the
second half of that same century, women's soccer made a
comeback, and since 1984, it has had its own World Cup
70 event. Now, many countries such as Italy, Denmark,
Sweden, Japan, the U.S., and Brazil are very enthusiastic
about women's soccer. So maybe, some time soon,
women's soccer will produce its own soccer legends of
the stature of Zidane, Maradona, Ronaldo, and Pelé.

---

venue = place where an event happens
varying degrees of success = sometimes successfully, sometimes
unsuccessfully
catch off guard = to surprise greatly
permit = allow
take a cue = follow the example
form a partnership = work together officially
dynasty = a ruling family
ban = not to allow or to officially forbid.

Second reading

C. Find these facts.

1. Give examples of how Brazil, Japan and Korea
   and women soccer players have influenced
   soccer history.
2. Give four reasons why Brazil's performance in
   the 1958 World Cup was unforgettable.
3. Give three reasons why Japan and Korea made
   history at the 2002 World Cup.
4. Mention two countries that supported women's
   soccer in the past and six which support it
   now.

Think about it

1. Why does the text say that women have had
   varying degrees of success in their attempts to
   be recognized as playing the game as well as
   men?
2. Why was Brazil's change of formation so
   successful in the 1958 World Cup?
3. Why was Japan's and Korea's organization of
   the 2002 World Cup an especially difficult task?
4. What kind of reasons might England, Holland,
   and Germany have had for banning women's
   soccer in the first part of the 20th century?

Vocabulary in context

D. Match the explanations or synonyms on the
right to the words on the left as they are used in the
text.

1. Line 3: dynamic	**a.**	very exciting and different
2. Line 11: struggled	**b.**	moved in great crowds or large numbers
3. Line 19: victory	**c.**	did the opposite
4. Line 23: flexibility	**d.**	beating (another team or other teams)
5. Line 26: attacking	**e.**	receive (as a guest or guests)
6. Line 26: reversed	**f.**	made great efforts in the face of difficulties
7. Line 29: flamboyant	**g.**	permanent proof
8. Line 34: host	**h.**	trying to score goals
9. Line 39: flocked	**i.**	lively, always changing
10. Line 55: records	**j.**	variety (of movement)

Discussion

D. Do women play soccer in your country? What
do you think about women playing soccer? Do you
think there will ever be mixed teams of both male
and female players? Why or why not?

Past perfect

A. Study the sentences and underline the verbs in each.

1. Brazil won the World Cup in 1958. They had never won it before.
2. Until 2002, the World Cup had always taken place in one country at a time.
3. As far as we know, women did not play soccer at the time of the Quing Dynasty, but they had played during the Donghan Dynasty.
4. After women's soccer had become very popular in the late 19th century, some countries banned the sport.
5. By the end of the 20th century, there were women's soccer teams in many countries, because women had struggled for years for their right to play the game.

B. Use the information from the sentences above to complete the following chart.

Happened in the past	Happened before another past event
1. Brazil won the World Cup in 1958.	1. They had never won it before.

C. PAIR WORK Complete these statements with true information about your life. Share the information with a partner. Then tell the class what you have learned about your partner.

EXAMPLE: *Until I started this English course, I had had serious problems with grammar.*

1. Until I started this English course, I ___(have serious problems with grammar)___.
2. By the time I left home this morning, I _____.
3. I went to bed at ___ last night after I _____.
4. Before I met my current boyfriend / girlfriend / husband / wife, I _____.
5. I relaxed a lot last weekend after I _____.

Past perfect

Simple past	Past perfect
The simple past describes an event (or state) which happened in the past. *Venus Williams won the Grand Slam at Wimbledon in 2001.*	When two events happen in the past and one happens before the other, the past perfect is often used to describe the earlier event. *When Venus Williams won the Grand Slam at Wimbledon in 2001, she had already won it once before.*

FYI

The most important tennis championships are known as Grand Slam tournaments.

Notes: The past perfect can be used with time words such as *before, after,* and *until* to make the sequence of events clear, but the simple past can also be used if the sequence is clear.

It is preferable to use the past perfect with *already, by the time (that),* and *when* meaning *before.*

Test yourself

D. PAIR WORK Decide whether you would complete the sentences with the simple past or past perfect of the verb in brackets. Then copy the completed sentences as one paragraph.

1. Before he (become) a professional soccer player, he (be) a shoeshine boy in his home town.
2. When he (join) the Santos team in Sao Paulo, the Santos fans (already hear) a lot about this amazing young player.
3. Although Pelé (never play) for such an important team before, he soon (become) the fans' favorite because of his flamboyant style and goal-scoring ability.
4. When he (retire) from professional soccer for the first time, Pelé (score) a total of 1,200 goals in 1,253 games.
5. Although he (be) sad to retire, Pelé (say) he (be) lucky because he (have) such a wonderful experience as a professional player.

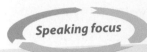

Speaking focus

Agreeing and disagreeing

The expressions below are organized from most formal to least formal.

Agreeing
- I agree with you completely.
- I feel the same way.
- You're right.
- That's for sure!

Disagreeing
- I'm afraid I have to disagree.
- I'm not so sure about that.
- I disagree.
- No way!

FYI

pie chart = a way to show information, using a circle divided into sections

Think about it

A. PAIR WORK Take turns giving opinions about watching or playing the sports listed below. Agree or disagree with your partner's opinion.

EXAMPLE:

> *I think golf is really boring to watch.*
> *I'm not so sure about that. If both players are good, it can be very exciting.*

soccer	tennis	volleyball	boxing	karate	basketball
baseball	swimming	athletics	gymnastics	ice skating	archery

B. GROUP WORK The government of your country has decided that elementary and secondary school students need more exercise! Starting next year, all students, both boys and girls, must participate in a sport at school.

You are on a committee in the Ministry of Sports, in charge of planning this new school sports program. You will decide which sports to include and how much money to spend on each sport.

You must choose at least four different sports, so that all students can participate, and you cannot use more than 50% of your money for any one sport. Record your group's decisions and show them in a pie chart.

Sport	%	Reasons
_____	____	_____
_____	____	_____

C. Now share your group's ideas with the class and explain why you chose the sports. Were the groups' ideas similar or different? Did any groups choose unusual sports?

A study by the U.S. government found that soccer is now more popular than baseball with American children between the ages of seven and eleven. More than three million boys and girls play in youth soccer leagues in the U.S.

5 Vocabulary in Detail

A. Read the text to help you understand the words in *italics*.

A new sports center has just opened in our neighborhood. The design is of the highest standard, and the center has contributed to making our neighborhood a much happier place. There are soccer and American football *fields*, with a *capacity* for seating 30,000 *spectators*. There are also basketball and tennis *courts*, and there's a skating *rink* which is open even in the summer. The most popular of all the sports, for both players and spectators, is soccer. Last week, our local team *played against* a French team, and it was so exciting. By *half time*, one of our *star players*, they call him Pelé the Second, had *scored a hat trick*, so the score was at 3-2 *in our favor*. Then, *halfway* through *the second half*, the *striker* from the opposing team caught us off guard, scoring a brilliant goal almost from the *halfway* line and *leveling the score* so we lost all hope of *beating* them. Fortunately, Pelé the Second *was on top form*, and just before the whistle blew, he scored again, *breaking* his own *record* of three goals in one *match*.

B. Find the opposite for these words in the text above.

1. players _____
2. a center back _____
3. play for _____
4. first half _____
5. full time _____
6. not at his best_____

C. Complete the text below with words from the text and your own words.

1. The biggest soccer stadium in our country is the _____.
2. On our national _____ , the _____ player is _____. His position is _____ and he is very good at _____.
3. I've got a friend who isn't into any kind of sport—either as a player or a _____, but she has other interesting pastimes; she _____ the piano and she walks a couple of hours a day.
4. Our coach always says it is very important to enjoy the sport you play and not to get too concerned about _____ records.
5. There is a skating _____ near my home.

goal	record	fun
match		

D. Use these words to form compound adjectives (noun + gerund) in the sentences below.

1. There's complete silence now on the court while Williams gets ready to serve what could be the *(match)*-winning point.
2. Pelé was popular not just because of his _____ -scoring ability but also because of his _____ -loving attitude toward life.
3. Michael Jordan is basketball's greatest _____- breaking player.

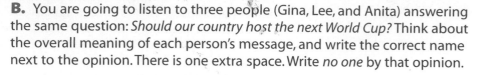

Before you listen

A. PAIR WORK What are some of the biggest sporting events in your country? Where are they held? Are they national or international? Have you ever attended one of these events?

First listening

B. You are going to listen to three people (Gina, Lee, and Anita) answering the same question: *Should our country host the next World Cup?* Think about the overall meaning of each person's message, and write the correct name next to the opinion. There is one extra space. Write *no one* by that opinion.

_____ says yes—because we can see some great athletes.

_____ says yes—because it will make our country famous.

_____ says no—because soccer isn't very popular here.

_____ says no—because it would be too expensive.

Second listening

C. Listen again. For each speaker, make notes of two things the person said that helped you find the correct answer in B.

After listening

D. What inferences can you make about the country you heard about?

E. GROUP WORK Should your country host big international sporting events such as the World Cup or the Olympics? Give your opinion and explain your reasons.

Test yourself

F. Look at the picture, listen, and answer the question. To find the correct answer, you must make an inference.

What will John probably do next?

a. Get help from the coach.
b. Take a picture of the team.
c. Go home to get his uniform.
d. Play soccer with his friend.

Listening strategy

Make inferences

Sometimes people don't state an idea directly. They imply it. To understand what they really mean, think about other information beyond just the words they say.

EXAMPLE:

> Chris: Do you want to play basketball tonight?
>
> Lisa: Hmm ... I have a big exam tomorrow.

We can make the *inference* that Lisa doesn't want to play basketball.

Justifying choices

Before you write

A. Work in small groups and choose from these lists the type of language (linking words, adjectives, phrases, expressions) that you would use if you were defending or justifying a choice you made and don't want to change.

It may be that ...	I am absolutely convinced that ...
There is no doubt that ...	I am not very sure whether ...
So perhaps, ...	She might be ...
First, ...	We will have to wait and see ...
Next, ...	highly skilled
unskillful	selfish
flamboyant	Finally ...

B. Now read this text and underline the linking words, adjectives, expressions, etc. that the writer uses to convince the reader his or her choice is the right one.

Man of the Match

There was no doubt whatsoever in my mind: Zinedine Zidane was *man of the match*. First, this fast, highly skilled player performed better than he had ever played before, scoring a hat trick in the first half. Next, he was totally unselfish with the ball, sharing it with his fellow players at every opportunity, and this contributed, in the second half, to the scoring of one more beautiful goal for the French team. Finally, Zidane was cool—with a relaxed and sporting attitude towards the game. Here is a player who never questions the decision of the referee even when that decision is dubious, so no one was surprised when the time came to name the man of the match, that it was Zinedine Zidane.

C. Look again at the words and expressions you chose in A. How many of the words you selected were used in the story? Why were some of them not used?

Write

D. Write a paragraph in which you justify your choice for Sports Personality of the Year.

1. First, brainstorm with your group and list the most famous sports personalities in your country. Talk about which sports they play and why these personalities are so popular.

2. Next, decide which personality is most popular in your group.

3. As you compose the paragraph, remember to convince your readers that you have made a good choice. Don't forget to list your reasons, using words such as *first*, *next*, and *finally* and to use positive adjectives to describe the person and his or her skill or ability.

4. Begin the paragraph with: *In our group we are convinced that the Sports Personality of the Year . . .*

Home work
Type a report
Which is main
sspoot in our
Country

A. GROUP WORK Design a mascot for a sports team you support, your English class, your school, university, or college.

1. Agree about what the mascot should be.
2. Decide how you will dress the mascot.
3. Draw the mascot.
4. With your group, present your mascot to the class.

Explain why you chose the mascot and why you dressed the mascot as you did.

B. GROUP WORK Work in small groups and decide which eleven international soccer players you would choose to form a World All-Star Soccer Team. As you make your decisions, complete the chart.

Player	Nationality	Position	Reason for choosing him

C. GROUP WORK Work with another group of students and compare your charts. Try to reach an agreement about the players. Share your modified chart with the class and try to agree upon players for the class's ideal soccer team.

D. CLASS TASK With the class discuss the following: Many famous professional soccer players cost their clubs a lot of money because of the high salaries they earn and the transfer fees the clubs pay for them. Do you think it is a good thing that there is so much money in the professional soccer game today? If you think it is good, think of all the reasons why. If you think it is bad, think of what you would prefer your country and other countries to do with the money.

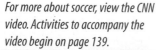

For more about soccer, view the CNN video. Activities to accompany the video begin on page 139.

Travel

Communication

Inquiring and informing about
    travel destinations

Debating the pros and cons of
    the tourist industry

Describing and discussing your
    preferences as a traveler

Grammar

Passive voice

Vocabulary

Travel and tourism

Destinations and tourist attractions

Verbs and nouns of
    transportation and movement

Skills

Reading for general and specific
    information: travel journal

Listening for important ideas

Writing: describing a process

1 Warm Up

A. PAIR WORK Describe the people in the pictures.

- What are they wearing?
- What are they doing?
- Which of these people
   do you think are travelers?
- Where are they?
- Which of these people do you think
   are tourists?
- What, for you, is the difference
   between tourists and travelers?

B. Put the activities and reasons in the appropriate section in the chart.

lie on the beach most of the day	take photos of local people
explore unusual places	have young children
eat local food	spend time shopping
take an interest in local culture	stay in good hotels
you are retired	talk to local people
you are young and unattached	have lots of time
need to rest and relax	have stressful jobs
don't mind discomfort	take tours of the most important
have short vacations	sights
go clubbing at night	travel light
care about the environment	

Tourist's activities	Reasons for being tourists
Lie on the beach most of the day	
Traveler's activities	Reasons for being travelers
	Have lots of time

Discussion

C. Do you think people might sometimes
choose to be tourists and at other times
choose to be travelers?

Reading strategy

Increasing your reading fluency

Read in chunks and note how long you take to read a text. Then try to increase your reading speed.

FYI chunk = a section or piece of something

Before you read

A. PAIR WORK Which of the following animals do we use as pack animals, i.e., for carrying heavy things? Which do we use for people to travel by? Which do we use in sports? Which do we use for their wool, milk, or meat?

Which of these animals do you have in your country? What do you use them for? Have you ever ridden on a camel? If so, describe the experience. If not, say what you think you would like or dislike about it.

| camel | cow | horse | donkey | goat | sheep |

First reading

B. Skim the text and decide.

1. Is the person a traveler or a tourist? _____
2. Is he or she enjoying this experience or not? _____
3. Is he or she alone or with other people? _____

Alashan Journal

Thursday, July 12: After a grueling week of travel by airplane and four-wheel drive, we finally arrived at the town of Yabrai Yanchang three days ago. Yabrai Yanchang is on the edge of the Alashan Plateau° in the part of the Gobi
5 Desert that covers the northernmost region of China on the border with Mongolia—that is, north of the Great Wall. For our trip into the Badain Jaran desert, which is located in the west of the Alashan, we abandoned° all forms of modern transportation and changed, in Yabrai, to a team of fifteen
10 camels and five horses. The Badain Jaran is remote°, **sparsely populated,** and famous for its enormous dunes°, or mega-dunes, as they are called. Walking across deep sand is always difficult, but these past few days have been especially hard, as the dunes have gotten taller and taller.
15 Today, when we reached the top of the highest dune— about 1,000 feet high—we turned and looked back. The **view** was amazing. Behind us, under a beautiful, bright blue sky, were vast° sand mountains in different **shades** of yellow. Our guide is a Mongol herdsman° who has al-
20 ways lived here. He entertains us with stories of life in the Badain Jaran. It can be very lonely here. His three children are being educated in boarding schools far from home, so he and his wife see them only in the summer vacation. Tomorrow, we will meet some more of the **inhab-**
25 **itants** when we go down into one of the valleys of the Badain Jaran.

Friday, July 13: At midday, we reached the top of a mega-dune, from where we had another fantastic view.

camel

cow

horse

donkey

goat

sheep

Below us was a rich, green valley with a small lake,
30 **glittering** in the sunshine. Sheep and goats were **grazing**
at the foot of the dunes, and there were camels and horses
near the shores° of the lake. We **trudged wearily** down
the dune toward two small mud houses near the lake,
where the only inhabitant of the valley, a woman of
35 seventy-two, lives. She is kind and **hospitable.** Her
existence reflects a surprising mixture of the ancient and
the modern. She serves us tea—just as her ancestors
would have done—but the water for the tea is heated on a
solar-powered stove outside her house. The sun's rays are
40 focused on the center of the solar collector, where the
kettle of water is placed. Inside the house, there is a
platform, made of earth, which serves as a bed and a
sitting area. In a corner, there is a **pile** of blankets, which
are used in winter when temperatures can drop to minus
45 30° C. In the roof, there is a hole for the chimney of her
stove, which she uses indoors in winter and outdoors in
summer. We sit and rest on the mud° platform° while,

outside, our hostess cooks a meal
of goat meat, potatoes, and wild
50 onions. With the food, which is
delicious, she serves us some of her
homemade rice wine. We find it
surprisingly strong and she smiles
at our reactions. Once she is out
55 or earshot, our guide leans over and whispers to me that
she drinks about a bottle of this stuff a day. ∎

the solar collector

plateau = very high, flat piece of land
abandon = stop using
remote = far from where people live
dune = hill of sand
vast = big and wide
herdsman = a person who looks after animals, such as sheep and goats
shore = sandy or rocky area next to the sea or a lake
mud = mixture of water and dirt
platform = high structure, like a table without legs

Second reading

C. Read to find these specific facts.

1. What and where is Yabrai?
2. How did these people get to Yabrai?
3. How are they crossing the Badain Jaran desert?
4. What did you learn about the life of the guide? Give at least three details.
5. Which animals live in the valley?
6. What did you learn about the woman who lives in the valley? Give at least three details. MUD
7. Where and what does the woman cook for the travelers? Goat, Potatoe)
8. What do they do while the woman cooks for them? Solar collector

Think about it

D. Give reason or reasons why:

1. they abandoned all forms of modern transport in Yabrai.
2. this guide is probably a good guide.
3. the guide's children have to go to boarding school.
4. the woman uses a solar collector to heat water.
5. she needs a lot of blankets in winter.
6. the person writing the journal is enjoying this experience.

Vocabulary in context

E. Find the words in the reading. Match the definitions on the right with the words on the left.

1. Line 11: sparsely populated
2. Line 17: view
3. Line 18: shades
4. Line 24: inhabitants
5. Line 30: glittering
6. Line 30: grazing
7. Line 32: trudged wearily
8. Line 35: hospitable
9. Line 43: pile

a. shining brightly (like a diamond)
b. welcoming to visitors
c. feeding on grass
d. the people who live in a place
e. with very few people
f. different forms of the same color
g. a large amount of
h. walked slowly and heavily
i. what you can see from a high position

Discussion

F. If you had the time, money, and other necessary support, such as a guide, would you choose to go traveling in a desert like the one described in the text or would you choose a different kind of experience? Give reasons for your preference.

Passive voice

Practice

A. Read these sentences carefully.

1. Nowadays, trucks and ships **are used** in most places for transporting goods.
2. However, in remote areas, camels, horses, and donkeys **are still used** as pack animals.
3. Most children today **are not educated** in boarding schools.
4. In some hot, sunny regions of the world, heat from the sun **is used** as a source of energy.
5. Solar energy **is not used** in cold countries.
6. Hot tea **is drunk** in vast quantities in Asia, even in the desert, while in Europe and the U.S., the favorite drink is coffee.

B. PAIR WORK Work with a partner and complete the following statements.

1. In Asia, elephants _____ sometimes used as a means of transportation.
2. There are special schools where the elephants _____ trained to work.
3. Goat meat _____ often eaten in desert regions, as goats survive well in difficult conditions.
4. In many desert regions and high plateaus, blankets, like the Mexican serapes, _____ worn at night, because it gets very cold in these places when night falls.
5. The serape _____ worn in Peru and Ecuador. The poncho _____ worn instead.

C. Write true statements about your country using the correct form of the verb in brackets and filling in the blank spaces with an appropriate word.

1. Several languages _____ (speak) in my country, but the most common language is _____.
2. Although _____ is the most popular drink in our country, _____ (drink) in large quantities, too.
3. In our country, _____ _____ (eat) every day. But _____ _____ (eat) only on special occasions.
4. In our country, most children _____ (bring up) by their parents, but sometimes, if

their parents are not alive, their _____ bring them up.
5. All kinds of musical instruments _____ (play) in our country, but the one people like most is the _____.
6. In some remote parts of our country _____ _____ (use) as pack animals, but most goods _____ (transport) in very big trucks.
7. Although games like _____ and _____ _____ (play) in our country, _____ is the most popular sport.
8. Houses in our country _____ (not make) of _____. They _____ (make) of _____.

D. GROUP WORK Discuss where these events are celebrated and when they are celebrated: Mother's Day, Father's Day, Halloween, Day of the Dead, Labor Day, New Year's, birthdays.

EXAMPLE:
> *Mother's Day is celebrated in many parts of the Western world, but it is celebrated on different days in different countries.*

E. Complete the text using the correct form of the verb in parentheses.

The growth of tourism on an international scale has brought problems, particularly related to tourism's impact on societies and on the natural environment. Past cases, like the overdevelopment of some coastal regions in Spain and poor resort planning in Pattaya, Thailand, (1) _____ (study) now in an attempt to develop a more balanced approach to the development of tourism. Some current concerns include game parks in Kenya, which (2) _____ (overuse), the Great Barrier Reef in Australia, which (3) _____ (damage), and trails in mountain areas of Nepal, which (4) _____ (affect) by irresponsible trekking. More and more, socioeconomic and environmental factors (5) _____ (include) in plans for new tourism projects. Also, more and more vacation options, whether they be called "eco-tourism," "green tourism," or "responsible tourism," (6) _____ (offer) for tourists and travelers who care about the environment.

Passive Voice

Forms of the Passive Voice	Some Uses of the Passive Voice
The verb *be* + the past participle of a verb	The passive voice is used without mentioning the agent, i.e. the person or thing doing the action, in situations such as these:
1. Trees *are being cut down* to make new farmland.	**1.** It is obvious or understood who the agent is. It is obvious that it is farmers who cut down the trees.
2. In some parts of the world, donkeys *are used* as pack animals.	**2.** The object of the action is more important to us than the agent. It is the donkeys that are important and not the people who use them.
3. Many reports *are circulated* on the Internet about the problem of the rain forests.	**3.** It is not known who the agent is. We do not know who circulates the reports.

Test yourself

F. Read the sentences and complete the chart with the *verb phrases* from the sentences.

1. In some parts of the world, rain forests *are being destroyed,* because the trees in the forests *are cut down* for firewood, the paper industry, or agriculture.

2. In other regions of the world, deserts *are being formed,* because the climate in these regions *is changing.*

3. When deserts *are formed* where once there was fertile land, the process *is called* desertification.

4. When desertification *occurs,* the region *is usually abandoned* by its inhabitants.

5. Many wild animals *are being affected by* climate changes, too. Their natural habitats *suffer,* so the animals can no longer survive.

6. Modern technology *is being used* to predict climate changes and prevent desertification.

7. Because some governments *care about* the rain forests, reforestation programs *are* common in many regions of the world.

8. Solar energy *is now being used* for cooking in some parts of the world and this *helps* to protect the rainforests, too.

Simple present active voice	Simple present passive voice	Present continuous active voice	Present continuous passive voice
occurs			are being destroyed

Speaking focus

Getting Clarification

Here are some questions you can use to get more information about something you don't understand.

What do you mean by . . . ?

Could you explain a little more about . . . ?

I'm not quite sure what you mean.

Think about it

A. Imagine that you and another student are going to take a three-day vacation together. Think of five things that you would like to do during this vacation.

B. PAIR WORK Tell your partner about the activities you want to do during your vacation and ask questions to get clarification about your partner's choices.

C. GROUP WORK You are the owners of a travel agency, and you are going to plan a 3-day vacation trip for the members of your class. Don't worry about the price, but remember that you only have 3 days, so you don't want to spend too much time getting to the destination. Work together to plan an itinerary and complete the list below.

Destination: _____

Activities:

Day 1 morning _____

afternoon _____

evening _____

Day 2 morning _____

afternoon _____

evening _____

Day 3 morning _____

afternoon _____

evening _____

D. Take turns presenting your vacation plans to the class and answer clarification questions from the students. When everyone has finished, vote for the best plan. You can't vote for your own group's plan!

Hawaii

Travel Australia & New Zealand

The number of vacation days that workers receive per year is very different around the world. A study by the World Tourism Organization found that Americans have an average of thirteen vacation days per year, Japanese get twenty-five days, Brazilians get thirty-four days, and Italians have forty-two days.

5 Vocabulary in Detail

line	Flight number	Time	Destination	Gate
	135	21:30	Boston	D43
	217	21:40	Cancun	B12
	4307	22:00	Amsterdam	D34
	52	22:10	Paris-DeGaulle	D36
	43	22:10	São Paulo	E44

A. Read the text below and write the highlighted words or expressions opposite the definitions on the right.

Most of us would agree that a tourist is not the same as a traveler, but the two do have some things in common. For example, to get to their respective destinations, they both have to go on a journey. If their **destination** is far away, both the tourist and the traveler may well prefer to fly, as a flight can take you where you want to go very quickly. It's once they arrive at their destinations that a few interesting differences between the two types of person begin to show. So, at the risk of generalizing a little, let's compare the two breeds.

If the first stop in the tourist's **itinerary** is the beginning of the classic tour of the most famous sights of various cities in various countries, he or she may tend to rush around trying to see, and take photos of, as much as possible before leaving for the next place on the list. You know the sort of thing, "If it's Tuesday, this must be Belgium." Other tourists, like yours truly, **head for** the beach, leaving it only to take a quick **trip** to the nearest shopping center or local **crafts market.** In the evenings, you'll find me, sorry, I mean the tourist, drinking in a bar, eating in a restaurant, or clubbing till the small hours.

In contrast, typical travelers tend to **take things at a slower pace.** Their aim is to get to know as much as possible about the culture and customs of the region. Local **means of transportation** are often preferred, even if this involves riding on a donkey or a camel. Sometimes, travelers simply prefer to see the region **on foot.** Travelers will tend, too, to prefer remote areas, which are seldom visited by other people, especially those darned tourists! Travelers are often particularly attracted by deserts and **jungles**, despite all the minor **discomforts**—lack of fresh water, insect bites, snakes, cholera, that sort of thing—that they might suffer in those places. Travelers also like to see wild animals in their natural habitats, and so a safari park is also a favorite destination. So what's it to be? Are you a tourist or are you a traveler? I know what I am. See you down at the beach!

1. _____	the place a person wants to travel to
2. _____	while walking
3. _____	to go immediately to
4. _____	the schedule for a journey or a trip
5. _____	do not rush
6. _____	place where local people sell the things they make
7. _____	buses, trains, ferries, etc.
8. _____	a short journey with a very specific aim e.g. to do business or to visit a friend
9. _____	things that can make your journey or your life difficult
10. _____	the opposite of a desert

B. Use these prepositions to complete the sentences.

> for   in   on   by   to   about.

1. Most tourists head straight _____ the beach when they get _____ their destinations.

2. Tourists like to travel _____ style, while travelers are happy to see the region on foot.

3. If the distances are great, however, travelers often go _____ bus.

4. Travelers like to get to know a lot _____ local people and their customs.

5. Going _____ a tour of as many places as possible in a short period of time is not the aim of the average traveler.

Listening strategy

Listening for important ideas

Here are some expressions people use to show how their ideas are related.

same idea

Besides, . . .

Furthermore, . . .

Also, . . . And do you know what else? . . .

opposite idea

On the other hand, . . .

But it's also true that . . .

Listen for these words to help you find the most important ideas.

Before you listen

A. PAIR WORK What are some decisions that people make when they plan a trip? Do you enjoy planning a trip? Or do you prefer having someone else make the decisions?

First listening

B. You are going to listen to two people who are planning their vacation trip to Belize, a country in Central America. Number their ideas in the order you hear about them. One picture is NOT discussed.

Second listening

C. Listen to the conversation again and list the positive (+) and negative (−) things that the man and woman mention for each tour.

	Positive	Negative
1.		
2.		
3.		

After listening

D. What do you think they'll do? Which type of vacation would you prefer?

Test yourself

E. You will hear a conversation between two friends talking about hotels. Decide which hotel each statement refers to.
A= Avalon B= Belmont C= Crown

It's not on the beach.	A	B	C
There might be a lot of noise at night.	A	B	C
There's a coffee shop.	A	B	C
It has a fitness center.	A	B	C

Describing a process

Before you write

A. GROUP WORK Brainstorm and list all the things you know about tea and the tea-growing process. Try to answer these questions:

In which countries is tea grown?

How many varieties of tea are there?

What colors does tea come in?

Is tea drunk in your country? If so, is it widely drunk or is tea drinking uncommon?

B. Read the following text and complete the notes.

There are more than three thousand varieties of tea, each with its own special flavor, color, and aroma. Just like wines, teas take their names from the regions where they are grown. Although tea is grown mostly in Asia, in such countries as China, India, Japan, Sri Lanka, and Japan, it is also cultivated in some African and Latin American countries. Teas vary in type according to the way in which they are processed after they are harvested.

Number of tea varieties:
Origins of names of teas:
Places where teas are grown:
Reasons why teas vary in types:

Black tea: Black tea is produced only in conditions of high humidity and warm temperatures. The leaves are harvested and spread out on the ground. Next, the leaves are rolled. Rolling frees the aromatic juices and causes a chemical process because of the influence of oxygen from the air. During this fermentation process, the tea leaves turn a bright reddish-brown color. After a few hours, the leaves are dried with hot fans.

Conditions for producing black tea:
First step in processing:
Second step in processing:
Effects of second step:
Color of tea after second step:
Final step in the process:

Green tea: As soon as they are harvested, the leaves are put into a large steamer and heated. This softens the leaves for rolling and means that the juices do not oxidize. The leaves are then dried again and again until crisp. They remain green in color.

First step in processing green tea:
Effects of first step:
Next step in processing green tea:
Color before, during, and after processing:

Write

C. Describe coffee processing. Write two paragraphs: (1) an introduction to coffee in general, and (2) a description of the most common form of processing. Use the Internet or an encyclopedia to collect the information you need.

A. GROUP WORK

1. In groups of four, choose a place in your country that you think a traveler would like to visit.

2. Work alone and pretend that you are a foreign traveler. Write a journal entry for your visit to that place. Try to see it through the eyes of a traveler.

3. Read your journal entry to the other members of your group. Discuss your entries and then write one entry using the good aspects of each entry.

4. Read this final entry to the class.

B. PAIR WORK Choose one of the roles below and act out your scene first with your partner, then for the class.

Role 1:
You work in a travel agency. A customer comes in and inquires about unusual destinations. Try to convince the customer to go to the Badain Jaran desert. Prepare to tell the customer how to get to this destination, what he or she would do after getting to the desert, and what things he or she might enjoy.

Role 2:
You are a enthusiastic traveler. You go into a local travel agency and ask the agent to suggest an unusual destination. He or she suggests the Badain Jaran. You know nothing about this place. Ask about the exact location, how to get there, the things you can do and see there and the difficulties you might face. Finally, decide if you are going to go or not and share the reasons for your decision with the travel agent.

C. CLASS TASK Discussion. With the class, discuss the following topic: Tourism is having a negative effect on many parts of the world.

For more about travel, view the CNN video. Activities to accompany the video begin on page 140.

Communication

1 Warm Up

A. PAIR WORK Work with a partner and describe the people and animals in the pictures. Discuss the ways in which they are communicating. Match these expressions with the pictures.

> Good morning! Absolutely delicious! Pleased to meet you! I love you!

B. Think about the different ways in which human beings communicate and group them under the three headings below.

> e-mail telephone postcards letters face-to-face conversations
> gestures hugging singing dancing facial expressions journal entries
> eye movements kissing shouting sign language
> short notes and memos

C. Discuss in what circumstances you would use each type of communication.

EXAMPLE: *I hug people if I have not seen them for a long time or if they are feeling sad and I am trying to comfort them.*

Oral communication	Written communication	Nonverbal communication

---

Communication

Discussing similarities and differences in types of communication

Describing the uses of gestures and facial expressions

Discussing the use of cell phones in public places

Grammar

More uses of the *-ing* form

Vocabulary

Communication and gestures

Animal noises

Metaphorical uses of animal noises

Skills

Reading for detail, inference, and cross references: scientific text

Listening for specific information

Writing: comparing and contrasting

 FYI hug = put your arms around someone

Reading strategy

Distinguishing between the main and supporting ideas

Try to locate the main idea in each paragraph and then look for the sentences that add information or details. These are the supporting ideas.

Before you read

A. What do you know about elephants and whales? Where are they found? What types of elephants and whales exist? What do you think elephants and whales might have in common?

First reading

B. Read the text and write the names of the animals which do these things.

1. Try to talk like human beings: _____
2. Sing when they are in love or looking for a partner: _____
3. Make extremely loud noises: _____
4. Talk to one another about everyday things: _____
5. Sing when planning a journey: _____
6. Communicate with other animals just like them: _____

Second reading

C. Find the word, words, or expressions to which these refer in the text.

1. line 8: *its* _____
2. line 15: *other species* _____
3. line 20: *one another* _____
4. line 34: *them* _____
5. line 41: *these amazing animals* _____
6. line 50: *other members of its species* _____
7. line 57: *it* _____
8. line 60: *some of which* _____
9. line 62: *some of these* _____
10. line 65: *that* _____

Great Communicators

*I*t is well known that certain species of birds, such as the parrot and the dove, are great
5 communicators. When the dove is in love, for example, it sings or coos incessantly to **its** partner. Whereas the dove
10 communicates mostly with other doves, the parrot communicates not only with other parrots but also with human beings, and its ability° to imitate and repeat human language has, over the centuries, been a great source of entertainment. It is perhaps less commonly
15 known that, in the animal world, there are **other species** which are just as good at communicating as the parrot or the dove. Both the elephant and the whale, for example, are great communicators, although they communicate in different ways and for different reasons.

20   Whales sing to **one another.** Even the rarest and largest of the whales, the blue whale, is often heard singing in the waters of the Atlantic Ocean. Whale song was discovered virtually by accident. During the Cold War° between the former Soviet
25 Union and the West, the Soviet government fixed hydrophones° to the bed of the Atlantic Ocean and used them to check when submarines° left and returned to port. After the Cold War, the hydrophones remained on the bed of the ocean, and scientists
30 suddenly began hearing this beautiful music, just like bird song, coming from the ocean. It was whales singing to one another. These wonderful recordings were shared with American and British scientists, and after two years of listening to **them,** the listeners
35 believed that whale music was used for mating and navigation.° Whale music is too low for the human ear to hear, but it can carry for thousands of miles; for example, a hydrophone in the Caribbean can pick up° a blue whale singing off the coast of Newfoundland. The

blue whale is the greatest of the whale singers, but
40 unfortunately, **these amazing animals** are still being
hunted, so one day their singing may stop forever.

Unlike the blue whale, the African elephant is no
longer in danger of extinction, as conservation projects
45 in East Africa in particular
have been very successful.
Like the blue whale,
however, the African
elephant loves to
50 communicate with **other
members of its species.**
Whereas whales sing,
elephants rumble°! The
noise that elephants make
55 when they are talking to
one another sounds just
like stomach rumbles, but in fact, **it** comes from the
elephants' throats and not from their stomachs. So far,
60 scientists have identified thirty different rumbles, **some
of which** are inaudible to the human ear; but others are
perceivable°, and **some of these** can be so loud that they

sound just like thunder. Each rumble has its own
character and carries specific information. For
65 example, baby elephants have a special rumble **that**
means, "I'm hungry. Can I have a drink?" Adult
rumbles can take the form of questions and answers,
such as, "I'm here. Where are you?" "I'm over here."
While studying elephant talk, scientists have also
discovered that females are more talkative than males.
Of the thirty known rumbles, females make six times
as many as males!

ability = skill, competence
Cold War = period in history when the Soviet Union and the West did not trust one another
hydrophones = apparatus used for recording noises under water
submarines = ships that travel under water
navigation = the science of planning sea journeys
pick up = record
rumble = low, powerful rolling noise
perceivable = something you can see, hear, or smell

Think about it

1. Explain why more is known about how parrots
and doves communicate than about how
whales and elephants communicate.

2. Explain why the Russians decided to share the
recordings of whale song with the Americans
and the British.

3. Why might it not be possible to record whale
song in the future?

4. How can we tell that elephants communicate
more than whales?

5. Explain why female elephants talk more than
male elephants.

Vocabulary in context

D. Find the words in the text and write the words
on the lines.

1. In paragraph 1:
   a. classification or grouping of living things,
   such as birds, animals, humans _____
   b. to copy what another person or animal does
   or says _____
   c. the beginning, origin, or cause of something
   _____

2. In paragraph 2:
   d. the place where ships and boats arrive and
   depart _____
   e. the bottom of the sea _____
   f. the task of finding a sexual partner
   _____
   g. to catch, and often to kill also _____

3. In paragraph 3:
   h. the disappearance forever of a type of
   animal _____
   i. cannot be heard _____
   j. chatty _____

Discussion

E. Have you ever had, or known someone who has
had, an experience with an animal that was a great
communicator? Tell the class about that animal and
how it communicated. What about human
communication? Do you think women or men are
better communicators? Give reasons for your
opinion.

3 Grammar in Detail

More uses of the *-ing* form

Practice

A. PAIR WORK Read the following text. Each of the verb forms in italics is used twice in different tenses. Put the simple form of the verb in the correct column in the chart.

> **FYI** belly = an informal word for the stomach or abdomen

The best vacation I have ever had was a safari in East Africa. I *remember* getting up very early every morning and going out in a jeep to see the wild animals. "*Remember* to bring your cameras," the guide would say as we were *preparing to* leave. The elephants were my favorites. There was one large female elephant that would *start* rumbling as soon as she saw me! I would get so excited I would completely *forget* to take pictures of her. One female lion *had started* to attract a lot of attention. She *enjoyed* lying on the ground with her belly up to the sun. Unlike other members of her species, she clearly *disliked* hunting and *preferred* eating only the very tiny animals that came her way. I shall never *forget* observing how happy she was. I must confess I am a bit like that lion. I *prefer* to take life easy. I don't really *enjoy* working all that much, and like the lion, there are things I really *dislike* doing. My boss is getting really impatient with me. "*Try* working a bit harder for a change!" he shouted at me the other day. "Or *prepare* to find another job." Sounds like a good idea. Maybe, I should *try* to find a job as a lion in a safari park!

Group 1	Group 2	Group 3	Group 4
Verbs that are followed only by the *-ing* form	Verbs that are followed only by the infinitive form	Verbs that are followed either by the *-ing* form or the infinitive with no change in meaning	Verbs that are followed by the *-ing* form or the infinitive form with a change in meaning

B. Complete the sentences using one of the verbs from the chart and the correct form of the second verb in parentheses. Don't forget to use the correct tenses.

1. If you are planning to travel in a desert, don't _____ (pack) a hat The sun is very strong.
2. I can _____ (walk) across part of the Gobi. What a marvelous experience!
3. Next time I go into a desert, I think I'd _____ (travel) by jeep. Walking is very tiring.
4. We used camels as pack animals. They were rather impatient and would _____ (spit) at us when they got tired.
5. I used to _____ (get up early) and _____ (walk) to the top of one of the highest dunes.
6. I _____ (take) a picture of a snake in the desert, but it was too fast for me.
7. My fellow travelers _____ (get up early) and would sleep rather late.
8. Sometimes, I saw snakes in the dunes. They would _____ (hiss) as soon as they heard me coming!
9. Although I had _____ (pack) my anti-snake bite medicine, I never got too close to them.
10. _____ (wear) in a hat in the desert. That should stop your headaches.

Interact

C. PAIR WORK In pairs, talk to one another about yourselves using the list below. Then tell the class what you learned about your partner.

EXAMPLE: *I will never forget passing my final exam.*

1. will never forget doing
2. often forget to do
3. remember doing as a child
4. must remember to do this week
5. prefer to do with friends
6. have started to do recently
7. enjoy doing at home
8. tried doing as a child

D. Rewrite the statements using the *-ing* form of the verb instead of the clauses in italics.

1. From the top of the dune, I saw several camels *that were moving across the desert.*
2. *When they were living in China,* my friends went to the Gobi several times.
3. *While they were studying whales,* scientists discovered that whales can sing.
4. The travelers heard a rumble *that was coming from the elephant's throat.*
5. I listened to the parrot *that was talking to itself.*
6. The herdsmen *who are living in this place* are very hospitable.
7. I thought it was a child *that was singing,* but it was some doves *that were cooing.*
8. *While we find e-mail very useful,* we also recommend face-to-face communication.

Grammar Summary

More uses of the *-ing* form

1. Always use the gerund form when these verbs are followed by another verb: *enjoy, dislike, finish, mind, suggest, avoid, can't help, can't stand.*	I can't help admiring parrots. They are so versatile.
2. Always use the infinitive when these verbs are followed by another verb: *decide, want, plan, prepare, agree, choose, hope, seem.*	They're planning to go on a safari this year.
3. Use either the gerund or the infinitive after these verbs when they are followed by another verb: *like, prefer, love, hate, start.*	She prefers to drink green tea. She prefers drinking green tea to black.
4. Use the gerund or infinitive with these verbs, but remember the meaning changes: *remember, forget, try.*	They can't remember meeting me before. I hope he remembers to come tonight.
5. Use the *-ing* form to replace a restrictive relative clause or independent clause to make your writing style more concise.	The lion that is lying in the sun is very funny. The lion lying in the sun is very funny.

Test yourself

E. Complete the sentences using the *-ing* form, the infinitive, or the relative clause.

1. I prefer _____ (talk) on my cell phone to _____ (send) e-mails.
2. Who is that man _____ (wave) at us?
3. While _____ (travel) in the desert, he got sick.
4. When I _____ (write) my journal, Paul arrived.
5. Did you remember _____ (pack) our sun hats?
6. The children will never forget _____ (listen to) the whale song recordings.

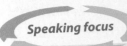

Speaking focus

Interrupting politely

In English, it's polite to let the other person finish speaking before taking our turn. Sometimes we need to interrupt the speaker to ask a question or make a very short comment. Here are some expressions you can use.

to interrupt: Excuse me, but …
Pardon me, but …
Sorry to interrupt, but …

to stop an interruption: Could I please finish my point?
Let me just finish.

after an interruption: As I was saying, …
Anyway, …
To get back to what I was saying, …

Think about it

A. PAIR WORK Do you have a cell phone? If not, would you like to have one? Tell your partner why. While one of you is talking, the other should interrupt. Use one of the expressions above to interrupt and ask a question.

B. Where do people commonly use cell phones? Are there some places where cell phone use is a problem? Discuss this with your partner.

C. GROUP WORK You are on a committee in charge of making rules about cell phone use. With your group, discuss possible rules. Try to interrupt other students politely once or twice. Prepare a short report of your committee's recommendations, including:

1. When it's okay to use cell phones
2. When people shouldn't use cell phones
3. When people must not use cell phones

in cars	in schools and universities	in restaurants and theaters
on buses	on trains on planes	

Add three suggestions for using cell phones politely. Take turns presenting your reports to the class.

D. What do you think about the other groups' ideas? In your opinion, is it okay for the government to make restrictions on cell phones? Is it okay for businesses like restaurants to make restrictions?

In the next ten years, the number of cell phone users in the U.S. is expected to increase from 125 million to 226 million. In Brazil, it will grow from 29 million people to 76 million, and in China, from 134 million to 575 million users!

5 Vocabulary in Detail

A. Read the following paragraph about animal noises. Find the answer to the questions in the text.

How do animals communicate? What kind of noises do they make? While lions **roar,** monkeys **chatter.** Cats **purr** when they are happy and **meow** when they are hungry. Snakes **hiss** to let you know they are dangerous. Mice **squeak** because they are neither big nor strong. Dogs perhaps produce the widest variety of noises. They **growl** to show that they are starting to get angry or impatient. When they are angry, they **snarl,** showing their teeth. They **bark** to warn you they are near, and if they are in pain, they **howl.** When bees fly, they **hum.** When they are busy, they **buzz.**

Which noise(s) in the text are:

fast and repetitive   not very strong or loud but very high   bright and cheerful

soft, rhythmic   long, dangerous and low   loud and angry

very loud   long, unpleasant and high

B. Use the correct form of the animal noise to complete these sentences, which describe noises human beings or machines make.

1. The boy _____ in pain when he broke his leg.

2. "Watch out!" _____ one of the gang. "There's a police officer coming down the street."

3. When she opened the door of the classroom, the children were _____ loudly.

4. When she told them she would punish them if they didn't stop, there wasn't a _____ out of them for the rest of the lesson.

5. When I heard the jet plane _____ into the night, I wondered if I would ever see my brother again.

6. "Take this coffee back immediately," _____ the customer to the waiter. "It's cold."

7. Could you switch that computer off? I can't stand that _____ noise it makes.

8. The students are so excited. They've been _____ around all day getting ready for the conference.

9. "You'll be sorry if you scream." _____ the thief, brandishing a knife.

10. The engine of our Rolls Royce _____ gently as we drove along.

C. GROUP WORK Work in groups and decide which noise best describes each place or situation. Then write sentences using "noise" verbs.

1. fast heavy traffic on a highway   **a.** squeak

2. a strong wind in winter   **b.** hum

3. wood floors that are old and need oiling   **c.** hiss

4. the radiator of a car engine that has gotten too hot   **d.** roar

5. an air conditioning apparatus   **e.** howl

Listen for specific information

Sometimes, we need to find only a few pieces of information when listening to a longer passage. Before listening decide what type of information you need.

Before you listen

A. Listen to an interview with a deaf man about how he uses technology to communicate. How might someone who couldn't hear communicate? Discuss this with the class.

B. PAIR WORK Read through C and D below and decide what type of information will be used to fill in each space—for example, a name, a number, a date.

First listening

C. Listen and find the information.

Guest's name?
When did he lose his hearing?
Guest's occupation now?

Second listening

D. Listen again and fill in the missing information about the way deaf people communicate.

1. Speech _____
   Understand what people are saying by _____ their face.
   Difficult because _____% of sounds are inside the mouth.
2. Internet _____
   Type _____ online.
   But have to wait for _____.
3. _____
   Works like _____ machine.
   Can read the message on a _____.
4. _____
   Used for longer messages.
   Can be connected with _____.
5. Closed-caption decoder
   Since _____, all _____ in the U.S. have this.
   It shows the dialog as _____ at the bottom.

After listening

E. CLASS TASK What new inventions could make it even easier for deaf people to communicate? Be creative. Devise your own.

Test yourself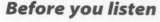

F. You will hear part of a radio program about how blind people read. Listen and complete the sentences. Some answers are more than one word.

Braille was invented in _____ **(1)**.
Computers have _____ **(2)** so that blind people can use them.
Braille is written on _____ **(3)**.
The dots _____ **(4)** from one to six.

7 Writing

Before you write

A. GROUP WORK Work in groups and discuss the ways in which the following forms of written communication are similar and the ways in which they are different. When and why do you use each form? Is one form faster than the other? How expensive is each form?

short notes to family and friends		e-mail messages to family and friends
postcards	journal entries	personal letters

B. Read the text about the similarities and differences between e-mail and cell phone communication. Then underline and list the words or expressions that establish (1) the similarities and (2) the differences between them.

E-mail Communication and Cell Phone Communication

Both e-mail and the cell phone are amazing inventions of the late 20th century that have contributed greatly to the ease of communication within and across nations. It would be hard to decide which of the two has been more beneficial to humankind. Like e-mail communication, the cell phone has contributed greatly to an enormous increase in the volume and efficiency of business deals. Similarly, the cell phone has been just as crucial as e-mail communication in helping family and friends to keep in touch even when they live far apart. The cost of using a cell phone and of an e-mail is similar, too. Both are quite expensive but for different reasons. With e-mail, it is the initial investment of buying a computer that is expensive; with cell phones, the cost of calls can be quite high. Despite the similarities between the two, there are also some major differences.

In the first place, cell phone communication is a lot more convenient than e-mail communication. You can carry a cell phone with you wherever you go; you can't do this with your PC. On some cell phones, you can access your e-mail, but that is not the same as having full e-mail and Internet facilities on your PC. Unlike e-mail communication, cell phone communication allows for a wide range of human emotions. The person you are talking to can tell from your voice if you are sad, angry, happy. Closely related to this is the fact that with cell phone communication, you know—again because of the voice—who you are talking to. In contrast, with e-mail communication, you might make friends via the Internet with a person who might be dangerous in some way. Whereas, however, health hazards are not so likely with e-mail, with the cell phone, there appears to be real a real risk that excessive use may result in the development of brain tumors.

Words or expressions for comparing	Words or expressions for contrasting

Write

C. PAIR WORK Work in pairs and write two paragraphs comparing and contrasting e-mail communication and personal letters as a way of staying in touch with family and friends. Try to use some of the words and expressions you listed in B.

A. GROUP WORK Work in groups of four. Pretend a foreign visitor is coming to your country. List all the gestures and facial expressions you use in your country that you think the visitor should learn. For example, do you have any gestures or facial expressions to communicate the ideas or to accompany the expressions listed below?

Maybe.	I don't understand.	Please, wait.
Come here.	Those people are very	Go away.
Don't do that!	rich.	Who knows / cares?
There's nothing left.	Everything's fine /	
Exactly!	wonderful.	

B. Pretend that the other three members of the group are foreign visitors and take turns teaching them one of the gestures or facial expressions you listed in A.

C. GROUP WORK Get into teams and try to find, in the word puzzle below, verbs for the noises animals make. Do this without looking back at the contents of the unit. Once you have found the verbs, write one sentence for each in which you say which animal makes the noise and when or how.

EXAMPLE:
snarl: A dog *snarls* when it is very angry.

Look for the words horizontally (from left to right **and** from right to left) and vertically (from top to bottom **and** from bottom to top).

M	H	I	S	S	T
P	U	R	R	N	Z
S	Q	U	E	A	K
I	K	M	R	R	L
N	R	B	A	L	A
G	A	L	O	D	T
X	B	E	R	Y	F

D. CLASS TASK Say whether you agree or disagree with the following statement and give reasons.

The use of cell phones should be strictly forbidden in public places such as restaurants, buses, subways, trains, classrooms, and libraries.

For more about communication, view the CNN video. Activities to accompany the video begin on page 141.

Review Your Grammar

A. Use the words in parentheses to finish the sentences. Put the verb in the past or the past perfect tense.

A: (Gloria, study) **(1)** _____ Italian before she visited Italy?

B: (she, study) No, but **(2)** _____ Spanish and the languages are similar.

A: (she, enjoy) **(3)** _____ her first visit to Italy?

B: (she, have) Yes, but **(4)** _____ a hard time with the language.

A: (she, already take) **(5)** _____ a conversation class at that time?

B: (she, not want) No, **(6)** _____ to spend the time and money to do that.

B. Use a passive form to complete each answer. Use the verb in parentheses.

1. **Q:** Did they have computers when you were a child, grandpa?

   A: (invent) No, _____ until the 1940s.

2. **Q:** How did people send messages across the U.S. before telephones?

   A: (use) The telegraph _____ to send long-distance messages.

3. **Q:** Do most countries have a telephone system today?

   A: (find) Yes, phone systems _____ in almost every country.

4. **Q:** What do you know about the first telephone exchange in the U.S.?

   A: (start) It _____ in New Haven, Connecticut, by Alexander Graham Bell.

5. **Q:** What is one of the important uses of cell phones?

   A: (use) They _____ by parents to keep track of their teenage children.

6. **Q:** Have computers affected the lives of many people?

   A: (affect) Everyone's life _____ in some way by the invention of the computer.

C. Complete each sentence in this story with the correct verb form plus a gerund or an infinitive.

1. (suggest, leave) My friends _____ _____ for the airport at six in the morning.

2. (dislike, go) I _____ _____ so early.

3. (forget, set) I always _____ _____ my alarm.

4. (remember, call) But they always _____ _____ me.

5. (can't stand, wait) I _____ _____ at the airport.

6. (agree, get up) But in the end I _____ _____ early.

High Challenge

D. Write the letter of the correct word or phrase in the story below.

1. By the time I arrived, the soccer game _____.
   a. had starting
   b. already started
   c. had already started
   d. started already

2. The team _____ by the coach.
   a. encouraged
   b. being encouraged
   c. is encouraged
   d. was being encouraged

3. I hate _____ late to a game.
   a. arriving
   b. arrive
   c. have arrived
   d. was arriving

4. I was late because my friends had to work _____ 9:00.
   a. already
   b. until
   c. by the time
   d. when

5. The game _____ early because of rain.
   a. ends
   b. had been ending
   c. ending
   d. was ended

6. The crowd _____ the stadium was very disappointed.
   a. was leaving
   b. left
   c. leaving
   d. already left

> **FYI**
> English language tests often include a multiple choice component. The items test your knowledge of grammar, as well as your familiarity with standard English usage. In this kind of question, it is useful to eliminate the options you are sure are incorrect first and then, if you are left with two options, choose the one which "feels better."

Review Unit 2

facial	hat	job	light
pie	star		

Review Your Vocabulary

A. Complete each sentence with a word from the box.

1. They displayed the results in a _____ chart.
2. I could tell how she felt by her _____ expression.
3. I don't need a lot of clothes, so I always travel _____.
4. Hilmi Kayan is one of Turkey's _____ players.
5. Yesterday Kayan scored a _____ trick.
6. Ellen has a really stressful _____.

B. Match each sentence with its communication goal.

___ 1. I have to take the bus because I can't afford to fly.

___ 2. I'm not so sure about that.

___ 3. When does the next train leave?

___ 4. I feel the same way.

___ 5. I need to arrive by 9:00, so I'm taking a 6:00 flight.

___ 6. I'd rather fly than take a train.

___ 7. No way!

___ 8. How much is a first class ticket?

a. agree
b. disagree
c. describe a preference
d. inquire
e. justify

C. Check the best response.

1. Do we have to hurry?
   ___ No, we have lots of time.
   ___ No, we don't mind discomforts.

2. How do you like it?
   ___ It's a means of transport.
   ___ It's absolutely delicious.

3. As I was saying . . .
   ___ I'm sorry I interrupted you.
   ___ To get back to what I was saying . . .

4. Let's tour all the important sites.
   ___ OK. I really care about the environment.
   ___ I'd rather take things at a slower pace.

5. The score is 20-10 in our favor.
   ___ I disagree.
   ___ That's great!

6. Have you checked the itinerary?
   ___ Yes. We have to head for the airport soon.
   ___ Yes. We need to rest and relax.

Review Your Speaking

Fluency

A. Make notes about a place you would like to visit.

- Name of the country (or city)

  _____

- How you would travel

  _____

- Where you would stay

  _____

- Descriptions of three things you want to see

  _____

B. PAIR WORK Describe your trip to a partner. Answer any questions your partner may have.

C. GROUP WORK Look at the photograph and discuss the gestures the speakers are using and what you think they mean.

F•A•Q I feel nervous when I speak to someone who speaks English much better than I do. What can I do?

You should try to learn some phrases that can help you begin or end a conversation, or show that you are paying attention. For example: to begin a conversation, you could start with something to interest the other person in asking you a question, such as "Yesterday I saw a great movie" or "I hate doing homework." To show that you are paying attention, you can use phrases such as, "Yeah," "Wow," or "That's interesting." To end a conversation, you can use phrases such as, "I've got to go now," "I have to . . ."

Review Your Listening

A. PAIR WORK When people are planning a vacation, how do they buy plane tickets and make hotel reservations? How can they get information about the places they will visit? Have you ever used the Internet to get ready for a vacation?

Listening 1

B. You are going to listen to two segments from a TV show about using the Internet to plan a vacation. What kinds of useful information can travelers find on the Internet?

C. Listen for specific information and fill in the spaces on these notes.

Two kinds of information the Internet is excellent for _____, _____

What you can find on web sites for tourist attractions _____, _____

Newspaper web sites have _____ and _____
A bad point of web sites that sell plane tickets: customer _____
Travel agents find hotels with _____ and _____

D. Listen again. What is the speaker's opinion? Think about the meaning and make an inference.

_____ You should probably use both a travel agent and the Internet.
_____ The Internet is the best way to make all your travel plans.
_____ Travel will change a lot in the future because of the Internet.
_____ Many travel web sites do not have very useful information.

Listening 2

E. Now listen to the second segment from the program and find the speaker's main points.

Problems with planning travel online

1. _____
2. _____
3. _____
4. _____

F. Listen again and mark the correct answer. You need to make another inference.

Nina Atkinson is probably
___ a travel agent
___ the president of an online travel company
___ a web site designer

Dancing

1 Warm Up

A. What are the people in the pictures doing? What country or region of the world do you think the people come from? Why do you think this? Is there anything in these pictures that surprises you?

B. PAIR WORK Use the first three columns of the chart to classify the dances in the list below, and columns four and five to indicate where the dances came from originally and whether they are group, partner, or solo dances.

waltz   samba   swing   merengue   line dancing   tango   quickstep
paso doble   rock 'n' roll   cumbia   salsa   hip-hop

Traditional	Latin	Modern	Specific region/country	Type
waltz			central Europe	partner

C. Use the chart to talk about the dances and to say whether you like this kind of dance or not.

EXAMPLE: *The waltz is a very traditional partner dance which came from central Europe. I like the waltz. It is a very romantic dance.*

Reading strategy

Using illustrations

Pictures, photos and other illustrations are used with texts to reinforce a message. Look at the illustrations to help you build up your expectations about the content of the text.

Before you read

A. What kind of dances do people in your country like to do? Where and when do people usually dance? Which dances do you like?

First reading

B. Skim the text. In the first blanks, check (✓) the topics mentioned and put an (x) at the topics not mentioned. In the next blanks, indicate the number of the paragraph where the checked topics appear.

1. the history of salsa: ___ ___
2. a definition of ceroc: ___ ___
3. the health benefits of dancing: ___ ___
4. some places people dance in: ___ ___
5. reasons people dance: ___ ___
6. some world-famous dancers: ___ ___

Time to Put on my Dancing Shoes?

Dancing comes as naturally to us as singing or speaking. And wherever I travel around the world I find people dancing. In fact, most countries or regions of the world have some form of dance that is typical to
5 that place. Dancing can fulfill many different functions, and people dance for different reasons. They dance to attract members of the opposite sex or to announce that they are about to go to war°, or simply to relax and enjoy themselves. And nowadays more and more people
10 who hadn't danced for years, or who had hardly ever danced at all, are taking up dancing because medical research has shown that, yes, you guessed it, "dancing is good for your health."

Researchers here in the U.S. studied the effects of
15 dancing on 400 cardiac patients in six hospitals in Texas. They found that those patients who took up dancing after their first heart attack reduced the risk of° another attack by 80%. I visited
20 one of these hospitals recently and one patient told me, "If I hadn't taken up dancing after my heart attack, I wouldn't have recovered so well. Now,
25 I'm fit, healthy, and happy!" Experts maintain that the benefits of dancing are not just physical, but also psychological. "Dancing allows you to forget your

30 problems," one therapist told me. "It's a form of escape that helps you switch off, forget your worries, and calm your mind." Fair enough, you might say. But you might be surprised to learn that regular dancing can be just as good for the human body as regular visits to the gym.
35 For example, salsa, a fast-paced, Latin partner dance, is great for toning° the hips, abdomen, and upper thighs, and it also burns about 250 calories an hour! My neighbor David is an enthusiast. "Salsa dancing is much more fun," he says. "If I'd continued working out
40 at the gym, I would have gotten bored. Also, you don't really get to meet people or make friends at a gym. At my salsa club I not only dance, I socialize too."

And this new-found interest in dancing for its health benefits seems to be a worldwide phenomenon.
45 Friends in China, for example, tell me that for some

people ballroom dancing in the local park has replaced the early morning jog or workout. And I read recently that in Japan, middle-aged businessmen have been seen on railway-station platforms practicing, not their golf swings 50 but their dance steps. In the U.K., thousands of people have joined ceroc clubs. Never heard of them? Don't worry. Neither had I. So I did a little research and found out that ceroc is a type of jive, a cross between° rock 'n' roll and salsa. Apparently, it has all the advantages of 55 salsa (but without the tricky footwork) and with the additional benefit that the music you dance to covers the whole range from 1940s swing and classic rock 'n' roll to Latin and current pop music.

The last time I was in France, I also saw this renewed 60 interest in dancing. There, where traditionally people have waltzed away their cares to the sound of the accordion, the "guinguettes" or popular dance halls are back in vogue.

Feeling brave, I visited one of these places one evening and chatted with the locals in my broken French. "Here 65 there are no barriers between the generations or social classes," one dancer told me. "We're all part of one big happy dancing family!" Later during a brief lull° between dances, one senior citizen told me: "This is the cheapest and easiest way to travel. Think about it—in 70 one night, I can visit Vienna, Buenos Aires, and Havana!" So, maybe it's time for me to put away those old sneakers and put on my dancing shoes.

---

go to war = to start fighting with another country or group of people
the risk of = the possible danger of
toning = increasing the firmness of
a cross between = a mix of two different things
lull = a temporary stopping of activity

Second reading

C. Read to find the facts that complete these notes.

1. People dance because
2. Physical benefits of dancing
3. Psychological benefits of dancing
4. Some countries where dancing has made a comeback
5. Some places where people dance

Think about it

1. Why has dancing made a comeback in some parts of the world?
2. Why might people who dance relax more than people who go to the gym?
3. What reasons might Japanese businessmen have for practicing their dance steps on railway-station platforms?
4. What age groups are represented in the French dance halls?
5. What did the Frenchman mean when he said he could "travel to Vienna, Buenos Aires, and Havana" in one evening?

Vocabulary in context

D. Complete these statements with a word from the text.

1. A person who is sick because of heart problems is a _____.
2. If we make a risk smaller, we _____ the risk.
3. Someone who has gotten better after an illness has _____.
4. If an activity has positive results, we say it has _____.
5. When we forget about work and / or our problems, we _____ _____.
6. If we use calories, we _____ them.
7. Starting with traditional, changing to Latin, and finishing with chart music can also be expressed as _____.
8. Another word for *obstacles* that prevent something from happening is _____.

Discussion

E. Which information in the text above did you find (a) surprising, (b) funny, (c) useful? Give your reasons. If you had to take up dancing for health reasons, what kind of dancing would you choose and why?

Unreal past (third) conditional

Practice

A. PAIR WORK Read the statements and write *positive* or *negative* after each, depending on whether it expresses a positive or negative view of a past action.

1. If those cardiac patients had taken up dancing sooner, they wouldn't have had such serious heart attacks. _____

2. If I hadn't joined the salsa club, I wouldn't have made so many good friends. _____

B. Read statements 1 and 2 again. Use those sentences to draw conclusions about *if* sentences and choose the correct verb tense of the *if* clauses.

1. In unreal past conditionals, the *if* clause is in:

   (a) the simple past   **(b)** the past perfect
   (c) the present perfect

2. The verbs in the main clause of unreal past conditional sentences contain *would / wouldn't have* and:

   (a) the *-ing* form of the main verb   **(b)** the infinitive of the main verb   **(c)** the past participle of the main verb

C. Complete the following statements with the correct tense and form of the verb in parentheses.

1. If our dance instructor _____ (be) so good, we wouldn't have learned so many new dances.

2. If generations of parents _____ (teach) traditional dances to their children, these customs would have died out.

3. If these ancient dances _____ (have) such varied social functions, perhaps we would not have learned so much about their customs and traditions.

4. If you _____ (practice) your waltz a bit more, you might have won the competition.

5. If Paul _____ (continue) to go to the gym, he would not have met Jenny.

D. Match the information on the left with the information on the right to produce statements of relief or regret. Sometimes there are two possibilities.

EXAMPLE:

   If I *hadn't stopped* quickly, we *would have had* a serious accident. *(relief)*

   If I *had stopped* the car more quickly, we *wouldn't have had* a serious accident. (regret)

1. I / stop / car / quickly
2. Brazilian team / change / soccer formation
3. members of the band / practice / so much
4. she / go / certified body piercer
5. that couple / have / more practical ideas
6. we / use / pack animals
7. tourists / get up early
8. I / hear / squeak
9. we / be / in form for our last trip
10. he / take up / dancing

   a. win / competition
   b. be / fit enough for desert travel
   c. see / so many wild animals
   d. traveling in the desert / be impossible
   e. take up / dancing instead of marriage
   f. have / accident
   g. get / infection / in ear
   h. have / serious health problems
   i. see / mouse
   j. win / 1958 World Cup

Interact

E. PAIR WORK Work with a partner and complete the notes below. Then use the interaction to exchange information. Tell the class what you learned about your partner's past.

Things I regret in my past	Things I am relieved about in my past
take up dancing sooner/ put on weight	take this course

EXAMPLE:

   S1: *Tell me one thing you regret about your past.*
   S2: *Well, if I had taken up dancing sooner, I wouldn't have put on so much weight.*

Unreal past (third) conditional

Type of conditional	Verb in main clause	Verb in conditional clause
Open (first) conditional *She may / will come if it doesn't rain* *She may/will come if it isn't raining.* The condition may or may not happen.	*will, may, should, can, must* imperative	*if* + simple present or present progressive
Unreal (second) conditional *If he were in my position, he'd understand.* *He'd go on safari if he had the money.* It is not likely that the condition will happen. It can refer to present or future.	*would* (abbreviated to *'d*) *could* *might*	*if* + simple past *if* + *were* (simple past subjunctive of *be*)
Unreal past (third) conditional *If I had been careful, I wouldn't have lost my ticket.* The condition cannot happen. It refers only to the past.	*would have* *could have* *might have*	*if* + past perfect

The conditional clause can come before or after the main clause in all cases.
I'd tell him if I were you.   If I were you, I'd tell him. If the conditional clause comes second, put a comma after the *if* clause.

Test yourself

F. Complete the interactions with the first, second, or third conditional tenses.

1. Are you coming to the salsa club tonight?
   I'm not sure. I _____ (come) if I _____ (have) the time.

2. Wow! Did you see that?
   Yes, if that guy _____ (stop) in time, he _____ (hit) that tree!

3. Just look at me—I've put on weight and I'm so out of shape.
   Well, if I _____ (be) you, I _____ (take up) dancing. It's such a nice way to get in form.

4. I hear Glenn's traveling in the Gobi again, but Sheila stayed home.
   Yeah, Sheila _____ (go) with him if she _____ (got) the time off work.

5. What do you think? Will we win the next match?
   I'm not so sure. If they _____ (put) O'Reilly in goal, I think we _____ (win), but this new manager is kind of dumb and he seldom plays O'Reilly.

6. Is Paula going to play soccer this evening?
   I think so. It depends on the weather though. She _____ (play) if it _____ (rain).

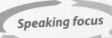

Speaking focus

Hesitating

When you need time to think of a word or idea, you can use these expressions to hesitate and show that you're not finished speaking:

Umm …
Well, umm …
Umm, let's see …
Let me think.

Think about it

A. PAIR WORK Dancing offers a number of benefits. It's fun, it's good for your health, and it's a good social activity. Talk to your partner and make notes about the benefits that the following leisure activities offer. While you are speaking make use of some of the hesitation expressions. In your opinion, which one of these is the best for children to learn? Why?

singing
art (drawing and painting)
playing a musical instrument
drama (acting in plays)

B. GROUP WORK Join with another pair for a discussion. The Ministry of Education in your country has decided that elementary schoolchildren should learn more about the arts. Your committee has been asked to design a program of classes that all children will take for four hours per week. Discuss dance, drama, singing, art, playing a musical instrument, or any other discipline and together, decide which activities children will do and how many hours they will spend for each. Prepare a group report. Explain your reasons and give examples. During this discussion try to use some of the expressions for hesitating.

C. Take turns presenting your reports to the class. Did you do any of these things in school? Did you enjoy them? Do you think they are a good use of school time? Why or why not?

In August 1983, Peter Stewart of Birmingham, England, set a world record by dancing for 408 hours without stopping.

5 Vocabulary in Detail

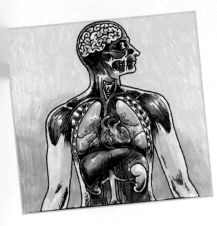

A. Read the text below and use the diagram to aid your reading.

We all know that physical exercise is good for our health. But different types of exercise produce different benefits. For example, walking is good for your legs, **hips,** and **buttocks,** and it is also very good for your respiratory system, because as you walk you get lots of pure air into your **lungs.** This in turn means that lots of fresh oxygen gets into your blood. Walking is also good for your **heart,** although more energetic aerobic exercise, such as all kinds of dancing, is probably more effective for conditioning this particular **internal organ.** Your **brain** is another internal organ that benefits from certain types of exercise. For example, research has shown that table tennis players are very quick thinkers because they have to think so quickly as they play the game. Of course, there are some **internal organs,** such as the **liver** and the **kidneys,** that don't benefit in a direct way from physical exercise. However, these organs benefit greatly from a healthy diet, free from too much fat and alcohol.

B. Put the words below in the correct section in the chart.

ankle heart cheek lungs navel eyes brain lips shoulder liver thighs knee stomach waist hips kidneys foot eyebrows

In the face	Internal organs	Upper torso	Lower torso	Leg

C. PAIR WORK Read the following examples and with a partner, discuss the meaning and the formation of the adjectives in italics.

1. She is *brown-eyed* and very *high-spirited.*
2. That man is *broad-shouldered* and terribly *flat-footed.*
3. Just look at that lovely *fat-cheeked* baby, and he's so *good-natured.*

D. Now complete the text using the words in parentheses to form the correct compound adjective.

Many **(1)** _____(long / forget) dances have come back into vogue because of the **(2)** _____ (new / find) benefits of dancing for our health. My brother, for example, who used to be quite **(3)** _____ (bad / temper) in the mornings, can now be observed smiling happily on the railway-station platform as he practices his dance steps, which he has learned at one of London's very **(4)** _____ (high / price)

dancing schools, where even **(5)** _____ (flat / foot) businessmen can learn to dance.

E. Combine the words from the box to create compound adjectives that describe people who:

1. have a very high opinion of themselves
2. care a lot about and help other people
3. can keep a secret very well
4. show no emotion; are not affected by others' suffering.
5. are practical and determined to get what they want
6. are reluctant to spend money

tight big hard warm cold head heart lip blood fist

Listening strategy

Guessing the meaning of new words from context

If an unfamiliar word is important, you will probably hear it again. So don't stop listening. Try to figure out the meaning of important words from other parts of the passage, just as you would when reading.

Before you listen

A. You are going to hear a radio talk about square dancing, a kind of American folk dance that began two hundred years ago. Do you know what kind of music is used for square dancing? What kind of instruments did people play in the past in your country?

First listening

B. Listen to the talk about square dancing and answer these questions about new words.

1. A *caller* is _____.
   a. an instrument　　b. a type of song　　c. a person
2. *Do-si-do* means _____.
   a. a good dancer　　b. a kind of dance step　　c. clothes for dancing
3. A *square* is _____.
   a. eight people　　b. very old music　　c. a party

Second listening

C. Listen again and complete the notes.

> Square Dancing in the Past
> Place where square dancing began:
> The first square dancers came from
> How callers began:
>
> Square Dancing Today
> Three levels of square dancing
> 1. mainstream (__ years)
>
> Good Points of Square Dancing:

After listening

D. What kinds of folk dance are popular in your country? Where and when do people do folk dances?

Test yourself

E. Listen to the short talk and answer the questions. Try to guess the meaning of unfamiliar words.

1. Who is speaking?
   a. a tour guide　　b. a teacher　　c. a dancer　　d. a traveler
2. What kind of performance will the listeners attend?
   a. dance　　b. music　　c. theater　　d. singing

An internet ad

Before you write

A. PAIR WORK Imagine you are going to go out for the evening—to a show, a concert, the movies, the theater. List all the sources where you can find information about the events that are happening in your city. Which of these sources do you prefer to use? Why? How do you prefer to get the tickets for the show? Do you book online or by phone, or do you buy the tickets on the night of the show? What are the advantages and disadvantages of each of these options?

> ### UPCOMING EVENTS
> San Francisco
> October 11th
>
> ### Michael Flatley
> ### LORD OF THE DANCE
>
> Now one of the most famous dancing troupes in the world, Lord of the Dance has been seen by a staggering seven million people around the world. Five years after Michael Flatley first brought the show to the world stage, the size and fame of LOTD continues to grow and spread. Today, LOTD consists of four groups: two performing in the U.S. and two touring around the world. This Celtic dance extravaganza has had great success in Japan, Africa, and Europe. Their CDs have gone platinum in Great Britain and Australia.
>
> Lord of the Dance offers an evening of truly spectacular dancing. More than forty dancers present a stunning interpretation of one of Ireland's most famous legends. Michael Flatley, the creator of LOTD, has brought together a team of top-class, specially trained young dancers. He remains the artistic director while overseeing all the troupes touring the world.
>
> **Ticket price: $50**

Write

B. GROUP WORK Work in groups of four. Read this Internet ad for an upcoming event and answer these questions together.

What information comes at the top of the ad?
What kind of information comes in the first paragraph?
What kind of information comes in the second paragraph?
What information is left to the end? Why do you think this is left to the end?

Design and write the text of an Internet ad for a famous group of artists you admire. They can be an international group or a national group; they can be singers, dancers, musicians, or actors. Refer to the text above for ideas on content and organization.

A. PAIR WORK Choose one of the roles below and act out your discussion first with your partner and then for the class.

Situation
You and your boyfriend or girlfriend are discussing your lifestyle. You have decided that it is time you got into shape, as you are not feeling very healthy, and you are living a very stressful lifestyle.

Role 1:
You want to join a dancing club. Decide which kind of dancing club you want to join and think of all the reasons why you have chosen dancing and this particular type of dancing as the solution to your problem.

Role 2:
You are completely opposed to the idea of finding the solution in dancing. Think of all the reasons why you do not want to learn to dance or join a dancing club and think of an alternative exercise program that would, in your opinion, be more suitable.

B. GROUP WORK Work in groups of three. Imagine that last weekend you all went out together and had a fabulous time, although you spent quite a lot of money. Choose one of the activities below and discuss all the reasons your night out was so fantastic and why you do not regret having spent so much money. Then form new groups and listen to the other members of the group talk about what they did and why they have no regrets. Who had the most unusual evening?

EXAMPLE
> *The food was excellent, although it was also very expensive. I had camel meat and it was delicious. If we hadn't gone there, I would never have tasted camel meat. Oh, yes, and we saw some famous people. If we hadn't gone to that restaurant, we would never have seen . . .*

No Regrets

1. went out for dinner to a restaurant and then went to a very expensive jazz club
2. went out to dinner to an expensive restaurant where many famous people go to eat and dance
3. went down to the river and had dinner and danced on a floating restaurant.
4. went to a show of famous group of modern dance artists that was running in your town for just one week, then had dinner in a restaurant

For more about dancing, view the CNN video. Activities to accompany the video begin on page 142.

C. CLASS TASK Some people were simply not born to dance and shouldn't even try. Discuss whether you agree or disagree. Give your reasons.

Landmarks

1 Warm Up

A. Describe what you see in each picture. Which countries or cities do you think are represented by these landmarks? What other kinds of structures or sights sometimes become landmarks for a country or a city?

B. PAIR WORK Use the names of landmarks, countries, cities, and types of landmarks in the word boxes to complete the chart. Then indicate in whether the landmark is natural or man-made.

Landmark	Country or city	Type of landmark	Natural or man-made
1. The Statue of Liberty	New York	a statue	man-made

C. Use the information in the chart to talk about these landmarks.

EXAMPLE: *The Statue of Liberty is a man-made landmark. It stands in the Hudson River at the entrance to New York City and is a monument to freedom.*

Victoria Falls   Great Sphinx   Louvre   Golden Gate Bridge
Temple of Angkor Wat   Petronas Towers   Taj Mahal   Seto Ohashi Bridge

India   Cambodia   Japan   East Africa   San Francisco   Kuala Lumpur
France   Egypt

mountain   waterfall   bridge   palace   temple   museum   skyscraper
a statue

Reading strategy

Understanding the meaning of a word in its context

To understand the meaning of a word, think about exactly what that word means in its particular context.

Before you read

A. Look at the picture. What do you find unusual or surprising about this bridge? Where do you think it is? Are there any special or unusual bridges in your country? Why do you think bridges often become famous landmarks?

First reading

B. Skim the text and write the number of the paragraph in which these topics appear.

a. the most important type of bridge for human beings _____

b. some historical facts about bridges _____

c. the reasons why bridges are useful in general _____

d. two very versatile bridges _____

e. details of a very long and strong bridge _____

Building Bridges

1. Leaving the state of Veracruz traveling northward along the Gulf of Mexico, you come to the Panuco River. On the other side lies the city of Tampico, Tamaulipas. The elegant Tampico Bridge stretches over 1,500 meters
5 across the river. High enough to let even the tallest ships pass underneath, the bridge is a beautiful structure and an engineering marvel. If you think about it, bridges must be among the most versatile° of all man-made structures. Before there were bridges, people, goods, and
10 vehicles had to travel for days or even weeks to find a safe place to cross rivers, fjords°, and canyons. Bridges join communities together and contribute to the economic development of the people on either side.

2. And to think that the earliest bridges consisted
15 **merely** of logs° which were placed across rivers. While these were fine for people—they were cheap, for one thing!—they proved useless for pack animals. Rope bridges, which are still used in some places like China and Peru, were invented next. Some of these were, and
20 still are, suitable for both people and pack animals; but leave your jeep behind, because these bridges cannot support **motorized traffic.** The next big step in the history of bridge building was the introduction of stone° and steel° as construction materials. It is from this time
25 that engineers and architects began to experiment with new and exciting designs.

3. Not only were these new bridges **capable of** supporting all kinds of transport—cars, buses, trains—they also became the **focus** of other forms of human activity.
30 The Ponte Vecchio in Florence, Italy, for example, is well-

known not only for its **exquisite** architecture but also because it houses
35 the **workshops** of the city's silver- and **goldsmiths.** The Charles Bridge in Prague,
40 in the Czech Republic, which was **erected** in the 14th century, is, with its thirty
45 statues of saints, one of the most beautiful bridges in the world, and it too is **a hive of activity.** Day and night it is crowded with artists and musicians who entertain the thousands of locals and tourists who cross the bridge every hour—all of them oblivious to° the fact that, when
50 the bridge was built, the builders used egg whites in the mortar° to make it stronger!

4. The Ponte Vecchio and the Charles Bridge are rare, historical bridges where people like to shop or take in a little culture, but perhaps the most impressive
55 bridge built in recent times is the Akashi Kaikyo Oohashi (as it's called in Japanese) or the Akashi Strait Great Bridge (by the rest of us). Opened in 1998, it is the longest suspension° bridge in the world. Did you know that suspension bridges are very functional, as
60 they are capable of covering longer **spans** than other types of bridges and they require fewer materials for their construction? They are also extremely elegant.

The Akashi Strait Great Bridge, which connects Tarumi
Ward in the city of Kobe with Awaji Island, is an
65 amazing 12,831 feet (3, 911 meters) long. It was
designed to resist° winds of 179 miles per hour (288
kilometers per hour), and earthquakes as strong as 8.5 on
the Richter **scale.** This is some bridge we're talking
about!
70   5. And some time in the future, they'll build a
bridge even longer and stronger than this one. But maybe
what we need more of is not bigger and longer
suspension bridges, but more of those invisible
bridges—the mental, social, and political bridges that

75 link people of different races, customs, and **creeds**
together. It is these bridges that can make the world a
more peaceful place.

versatile = useful in many ways	oblivious to = not knowing
fjord = narrow area of sea which goes far into high land	mortar = mixture used to hold stone or brick together
log = tree trunk that has been cut	suspension = hanging
stone = piece of rock	resist = to remain strong even
steel = a strong metal	when there is an opposing force …

Second reading

C. Find these specific details.

1. Two regions joined by the Tampico Bridge in
Mexico _Veracruz y tampico tamaulipas_

2. Main advantage of the earliest bridges
They were cheap and simple

3. Main disadvantage of the earliest bridges
These were useless for pack animals

4. Countries where rope bridges are still used
Peru and China

5. Reasons why bridges became stronger and
more versatile _The introduction of stone and steel_

6. Country in which you can see the Ponte
Vecchio _in Italy_

7. City in which you can cross the Charles Bridge
Prague

8. Country in which you can find the longest
suspension bridge _Japan_

Think about it

1. In what ways do bridges contribute to the
development of a country or region?

2. Why were pack animals unable to cross the
earliest bridges?

3. What do the Ponte Vecchio and the Charles
Bridge have in common?

4. Why might some people be afraid to cross the
Charles Bridge?

5. How do you know that the Akashi Strait Great
Bridge is extremely strong?

6. Why do the invisible bridges made by human
beings make the world a better place?

Vocabulary in context

D. Choose a word or expression from the list that
means the same as a word from the text.

a person who makes jewelry	only	center
place where people make things		distances
vehicles with engines	religions	build
very delicate	a system of measurement	
had the power to	a busy place	

1. Line 15: merely _____
2. Line 22: motorized traffic _____
3. Line 27: (were) capable of _____
4. Line 29: focus _____
5. Line 32: exquisite _____
6. Line 35: workshop _____
7. Line 37: goldsmith _____
8. Line 42: erect _____
9. Line 46: a hive of activity _____
10. Line 60: spans _____
11. Line 68: scale _____
12. Line 75: creeds _____

Discussion

E. Which of the four famous bridges mentioned in
the text would you like to visit? Give reasons for
your choice, and describe what you think you would
see on and from that particular bridge.

Passive voice: simple past

Practice

A. PAIR WORK Read the pairs of sentences below and indicate whether they are in the passive or active voice.

1. **a.** The logs were placed across rivers. _____
   b. These early bridges were suitable for human beings. _____
2. **a.** Rope bridges were invented next. _____
   b. Rope bridges are still in use in certain parts of the world today. _____
3. **a.** Stone and steel bridges were capable of supporting motorized traffic. _____
   b. They also became the focus of other activities. _____
4. **a.** The Charles Bridge was erected in the 14th century. _____
   b. Modern technology was not used in the construction of the Charles Bridge. _____
5. **a.** Egg whites were definitely not used in the construction of the Akashi Strait Great Bridge. _____
   b. This bridge was designed to resist winds of 179 miles per hour. _____

B. Complete the text with the correct form of the verbs in parentheses.

1. The Eiffel Tower in Paris _____ (design) by the famous French engineer Gustave Eiffel and _____ (complete) in 1889.
2. The statues of Easter Island _____ (build) between the 10th and 16th century, but they _____ (discover) until 1722 by the Dutch explorer Jakob Roggeveen.

3. The Potala Palace in Lhasa, Tibet, _____ (erect) in the late 17th century.
4. The Watts Towers in Los Angeles _____ (construct) from junk by Sam Rodia.
5. Although explorers had speculated about their location, the Victoria Falls _____ (discover) until 1855 by David Livingstone.

C. Read the two examples below. Why do you think Example 2 is preferable to Example 1? Rewrite the text about the United Nations Organization (U.N.) by reducing or combining some of the passive voice sentences, where appropriate.

EXAMPLE 1: *The Eiffel Tower was designed by Gustave Eiffel. It was completed in 1889.*

EXAMPLE 2: *Designed by Gustave Eiffel, the Eiffel Tower was completed in 1889.*

The United Nations Organization (U.N.) was founded in 1945. It was established with the aim of building bridges between nations and generally, of contributing to world peace. Initially, only fifty nations joined the organization, but eventually many more nations were admitted. The celebration of the 55th anniversary of the founding of the U.N. was attended by representatives of most of the member nations of the U.N. The anniversary was celebrated in 2000. Many famous people give a lot of their free time to working as messengers of peace for the U.N. Muhammad Ali was appointed Messenger of Peace in 1998. He has traveled all over the world trying to promote better understanding between nations.

Interact

D. PAIR WORK Read these two sentences and discuss why the person who performs the action (the agent) is used in Example 1 and not in Example 2. Then look at the sentences below. With a partner, discuss: Does the information about the agent (the person or thing that performs the action) seem to add something important to the sentence.

EXAMPLE 1: *The Eiffel Tower was designed by Gustave Eiffel.*

EXAMPLE 2: *The Eiffel Tower was completed in 1889.*

1. The Association of South East Asian nations (ASEAN) was founded by a group of nations in 1967.
2. The Magic Flute was composed by Mozart and performed for the first time by a group of musicians in 1791.

2. The Magic Flute was composed by Mozart and performed for the first time by a group of musicians in 1791.
3. Many of the workers who made the first attempt to build the Panama Canal were killed by tropical diseases.
4. The team was very well trained by their trainers before participating in the World Cup.
5. These jeans were made by workers in Indonesia.
6. During our journey through the desert, our food, clothes, and other possessions were transported by a team of pack animals.
7. The last time I went on a trip, my passport was stolen by a thief.
8. Veronica was advised by her psychoanalyst to take up dancing as a form of relaxation.

Passive voice: simple past

Passive voice: simple past	Examples
The simple past in the passive voice is formed with the simple past of the verb *be* and the past participle.	*The Taj Mahal was completed in 1648.* *I wasn't told about the party.*

Nonuse of the agent when:	
The agent is not important. The agent is not known. The agent is obvious. The speaker wants to conceal the agent.	*The letter was delivered yesterday.* *My suitcase was stolen.* *He was elected president in 2002.* *A serious mistake was made last week.*

Use of agent when:	
The proper name of the agent is important. To emphasize the doer or cause of the action.	*In 2002, the Best Actress Oscar was won by Halle Berry.* *They were attacked by a pack of wild dogs.*

Test yourself

E. Complete the dialog with correct tense, form, and voice of the verbs in brackets and decide whether the agents are necessary or unnecessary.

Waiter: Excuse me, would you like to have a drink while your table **(1)** _____ (prepare.)

Customer 1: Yeah, I'd like a fresh orange juice.

Customer 2: Hmm, is the juice fresh?

Waiter: Yes, our orange juice **(2)** _____ (make) with oranges from our own garden. They **(3)**_____ (pick) by some workers every morning.

Customer 2: Okay, then a fresh orange juice for me too.

Customer 1: So, go on . . . you **(4)** _____ (tell) me last week that your job is safe?

Customer 2: Yeah, can you believe it! And just a month ago, I **(5)** _____ (advise) to go look for another position.

Customer 1: Do you get to travel a lot in your job?

Customer 2: Yes, I do. I **(6)** _____ (send) to the Middle East by my company next month. And I was in Asia twice last year.

4 Speaking

Speaking focus

Managing the topic

Sometimes in a discussion, people start talking about a different topic. To return to the main topic politely, you can use these expressions:

To get back to what we were talking about, . . . As we were saying, . . . Let's go back to . . .

Think about it

A. PAIR WORK Talk about these pictures with your partner. Do you know where they are? What do you think the shapes mean? If you get off the main topic, use one of the expressions from the box.

B. GROUP WORK The city government is planning a new park in your city and has asked your committee to design a monument with a time capsule inside. The monument will be a symbol of life in your country now, and it will be fifteen feet tall. Work together to design the monument. Use some of the expressions above to help your group keep to the main topic.

1. Choose a shape (one of these or a different shape) and decide what the shape represents.

2. Choose three symbols to put on the outside to show your hopes for the future.

3. Choose ten things to put inside the "time capsule" to be opened one hundred years from now. These things should show what life is like today. Remember, the monument will be fifteen feet tall, so all the objects have to fit.

4. With the group, draw a picture of your monument on a large piece of paper.

C. Take turns telling the class about your monument and the things inside the time capsule. Explain your decisions.

A time capsule is a container of things that are stored for a long time (for example, 100 years). It gives a picture of life at the time it was made. When a time capsule from 1873 was opened in Rochester, New York, in 1999, people found advertising, coins, newspapers, letters, and photographs.

5 Vocabulary in Detail

A. PAIR WORK Read the text. Then, in pairs, discuss the possible meanings of the highlighted words.

Some countries or parts of the world become world famous because of their **geographic features.** For example, Norway is famous for its **fjords**—long, narrow strips of sea that **penetrate** high land and that have steep **cliffs** on either side. Northern India, on the other hand, is famous for its **majestic** mountains, the Himalayas, which **rise** to such enormous heights that the **peaks** of the particular **range of mountains** can be seen from a great distance in many neighboring countries. In contrast, it is probably the **pampas** or expansive, flat **plains, stretching** the full length of the country, that make Argentina well-known, whereas countries in the Middle East, like Saudi Arabia, are famous for their vast, **arid** deserts that **stretch** for thousands of miles with only the occasional **oasis.** Countries like Brazil and Canada are well-known for their impressive **water formations.** It is **natural landmarks,** like the **waterfalls** at Iguaçu and Niagara, that attract thousands of tourists to these countries every year. Other natural landmarks are **canyons,** where powerful rivers have flowed for centuries, forming these deep cracks in the earth.

B. Create a chart with adjectives and verbs that go with the names of the natural landmarks in the box.

| fjords cliffs mountains |
| plains deserts waterfalls |
| canyons rivers |

Natural Landmarks	Adjectives	Verbs
1. fjords	(a) deep (b) long (c) narrow	penetrate

C. PAIR WORK Use the vocabulary from your chart to talk about the geography and natural landmarks in your country and in other parts of the world that you know about

EXAMPLES:
1. *The Andes is a majestic mountain range in South America that stretches from Colombia in the north to Chile in the south.*
2. *Mount Everest is a world-famous natural landmark in the Himalayas that rises to an impressive height of 29,028 feet.*

D. Read the sentences below and note the use of idioms. Select which of the two interpretations on the right is the correct one.

1. That pop singer is *at the peak of* her career.
   a. at the best moment of
   b. at the worst moment of

2. That course was incredibly *arid.*
   a. interesting
   b. boring

3. It is time *to bridge the gap* between rich and poor.
   a. reduce the differences
   b. describe the differences

4. Forget about it! *It's water under the bridge.*
   a. It happened very quickly.
   b. It cannot be changed.

5. The soccer players were *in peak condition* at the World Cup.
   a. very nervous
   b. very healthy

Listening strategy

Use visual clues

Always use visual clues that are available to you, such as photographs, body language, and facial expressions. This will help you to obtain more information about the subject.

Before you listen

A. PAIR WORK Look at the buildings in the pictures below and describe them. Do you think they look good? Why or why not?

First listening

B. You are going to hear an announcement for a radio series about three of the buildings in the pictures. Think about the words you used to describe them in A. Then listen and number the buildings. One picture will not have a number.

Second listening

C. Listen again and find two different opinions, one positive and one negative, about each building.

After listening

D. Do you agree with any of the opinions in C? What do you think about some of the new buildings in your city or country?

Test yourself

E. Look at the picture and think about how to describe it. You will hear four statements. Write the letter of the one that describes the picture.

Text for a travel brochure

Before you write

A. GROUP WORK In groups of four, discuss the most famous natural and man-made landmarks in your country. How many of them have you seen or visited? Which are your favorites? Give reasons for your decisions.

B. Read the paragraphs below and answer the questions. Discuss your answers with your group.

Built sometime between 2575 and 2465 B.C., the Great Sphinx is one of the most impressive of the Egyptian landmarks. The Sphinx was a mythological creature with a lion's body and a human head and was used as a kind of portrait to represent the kings of Egypt. The Great Sphinx was long believed to be a likeness of King Khafre.

While you may marvel at the wonders of the monuments made by man, you will surely be completely amazed at the natural beauty of the River Nile, which is the source of Egypt's economic and cultural development. It is also believed that the warm, generous and friendly character of the Egyptian people is greatly influenced by the river, as it flows gently and quietly through this rich, fertile land.

Which text is about a man-made landmark and which is about a natural landmark? How does the writer introduce the first text? How is the second text introduced? Why are these introductions expressed in these ways? What does the author tell us after each introduction? Where and why is the passive voice used in the texts?

Write

C. Write two paragraphs for a travel brochure, one about a natural landmark and the other about a man-made landmark in your country. Decide how you will introduce and develop each text and if, why, and where you will use the passive voice.

A. PAIR WORK A friend of one of your friends will be in your country on a business trip and has one free day. Your friend has asked you to show this person some of the landmarks, natural or man-made, in your town, city or region on that day.

> • Work alone and decide what you would show the visitor and why.
> • With a partner, compare your decisions and try to reach a compromise if you have chosen different landmarks.

B. GROUP WORK You are going to be tourist guides for three important man-made landmarks in your country.

> • In groups of three, choose the three landmarks and allocate one to each person.
> • Work alone and prepare a short oral presentation of the history, use, etc., of your landmark.
> • In your groups, listen to each other's presentations and help one another to improve them.
> • Pretend the other members of the class are tourists, and in your groups of three, take turns at taking them on a tour of your landmarks.

C. CLASS TASK Make a list of some places in the world where two communities or two countries need to understand each other better. What kinds of problems are preventing these communities or countries from building the human bridges that would lead to better relationships between them? Discuss ways in which you think they could resolve their differences and live in peace.

For more on landmarks, view the CNN video. Activities to accompany the video begin on page 142.

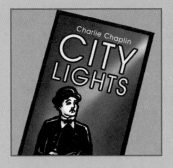

Movies

1 Warm Up

A. GROUP WORK Look at the movie posters and discuss the kinds of movies you think are advertised in each poster.

• When do you think each movie was made?

• Why do you think this? Have you seen any of these movies?

• What types or genres of movie do you like best?

B. In the same groups, match the names of the movies with the movie genres and the name or names of the movie director. Then use the information to talk about each movie.

EXAMPLE: *E.T. is a science fiction fantasy. It was released in 1982 and was directed by Steven Spielberg.*

E.T. (1982)	science fiction movie	Billy Wilder
Fargo (1996)	thriller	Orson Welles
Frankenstein (1931)	romantic comedy	Steven Spielberg
Citizen Kane (1941)	fictional biography	Alfred Hitchcock
An American in Paris (1951)	crime drama	Joel Cohen
Psycho (1960)	horror movie	James Whale
Some Like It Hot (1959)	romantic musical	Vincente Minnelli

C. CLASS TASK Look again at the names of the directors in the box. Brainstorm with the class and list the names of other famous movie directors you know. List and discuss some of their most famous movies.

> **FYI**
>
> Genre is a word of French origin. It is pronounced /ʒən'rə/ which sounds like ZHAN-RUR. It means a specific type of text, music, film, or art, grouped according to a style or subject.
>
> EXAMPLE:
> *Comedy is a very different genre from horror.*

Reading strategy

Noticing dates in a text with historical information

Look for dates in the text and try to follow the general chronological sequence of events. This will help you understand the text better.

Before you read

A. GROUP WORK Discuss when you think the very first movies were made, what problems the early movie makers had, and the ways in which movies today are different from these movies.

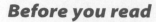

First reading

B. Scan the text to find out if these statements are true or false. If they are false, correct them. If they are true, identify the information in the text that supports them.

1. A U.S. citizen was the first to project a movie to an audience. *France* *False*
2. The first movies ever projected were about real people and things. *true*
3. Thomas Edison, the famous American inventor, had always believed in the future of movies. *false*
4. *The Great Train Robbery* was the first movie ever to tell a story. *False*
5. The first movies to tell a story were projected in movie theaters. *False* *Fal*
6. The first movie posters contained the names of the principal movie stars. *fal*
7. Sound was added to movie production in the 1920s. *true*
8. During the Great Depression of the early 1930s, people lost their enthusiasm for the movies. *False*

Landmarks in Movie-making

No one is really sure who produced and projected° a movie, or motion picture as they were originally called, for the very first time, but in the late 19th century and the early 20th century, many people in different parts
5 of the world, especially in France and the United States, were working hard on the **relevant** inventions°. As a result, in France 1895, the Lumière brothers became the first people ever to project a movie on a screen to an audience. The film consisted of scenes of workers
10 leaving the Lumière factory. This motivated Thomas Edison, the famous American inventor, to take a keener° interest in motion pictures. Unlike the French inventors, he had initially considered motion pictures a passing fad, which would soon fade.
15   Subsequently, in 1896, Edison presented his first film show in New York City. The program consisted of scenes of a dancer and of waves rolling on a beach. Up to this point, movies were nothing more than short presentations of actual events and the novelty° of the initial showings
20 soon wore off. Audiences began to grow bored and people generally lost interest in the movie industry. Then, in 1899, George Méliès, a Frenchman who had been a magician, produced the first motion picture that told a story. He filmed hundreds of fairy tales° and science

25 fiction stories, and once again, interest in motion pictures **flourished.** The first American movie that
30 used modern film techniques to tell a story was *The Great Train Robbery* —an eleven-minute movie describing a train robbery and
35 the capture° of the robbers. This movie was such a great hit that it led to the establishment in 1905 of nickelodeons, the forerunners of movie theaters. Nickelodeons were stores that were converted into movie theaters by simply adding chairs, and where the
40 cost of **admission** was five cents. By 1910, however, business was so good that the nickelodeons were soon being replaced by proper movie theaters.
    As the number of movie-making companies grew, competition became **stiff** and advertising **paramount.**
45 At the beginning of the 20th century, the first movie posters had to be designed so that the majority of the general public could understand them. Since many people were still **illiterate** in the early years of the

1900s, the posters contained few words. Most
50 surprisingly perhaps, while they provided the name of the movie and the times and place of each showing, they did not give the names of the movie stars.

Many of the actors in the early movies chose to remain anonymous as they were ashamed° that people
55 would find out they were participating in this new **medium.** Furthermore, film producers preferred not to name the actors, as they feared that if the actors became famous, they would **demand** higher salaries. By 1910, however, it became clear that it was interest in the actors
60 as much as the movies themselves that brought a great increase in audience numbers. Suddenly, posters had to be designed with consideration given to the stars, and thus began the **age** of the great movie star. When in the mid-1920s, sound was added to movie production, the
65 popularity of these new "talkies," as they were called, combined with the growing fascination with the movie

stars, was so great that movie **attendance** increased from 60 million in 1927 to 110 million in 1929 and even the Great Depression of the 1930s failed to
70 **dampen** the enthusiasm of the movie-crazy public. On the contrary, such was the public's need to escape from the reality of their daily lives that producers found ways to cut the costs of production so that the price of admission could be adjusted° to the moviegoers'
75 **meager** budgets.

> project = make an image appear on a screen or surface
> invention = something useful created by someone, such as a new machine or system
> keen = strong, intense
> novelty = newness and attractiveness
> fairy tale = children's story with imagined facts and people
> capture = catch by force
> ashamed = unhappy and uncomfortable about something
> adjust = change so that it suits

Second reading

C. Read to find these facts.

1. What kinds of things did people see when they first went to the movies? *Pictures*

2. How did Georges Méliès help to revive interest in movies? *He Produced the Motion Pictures*

3. What exactly were the first movie theaters?

4. What were the main characteristics of the first movie posters?

5. What two things helped movies to become so popular in the 1920s?

Think about it

1. Why do you think Edison began to take a keener interest in movies than he had done at first?

2. Why do you think *The Great Train Robbery* was a success?

3. What is another word for a five-cent U.S. coin?

4. Why do you think actors were initially ashamed to admit that they acted in movies?

5. Why was the design of movie posters changed after 1910?

6. Why do you think the general public needed to "escape from the reality of their daily lives" during the Great Depression?

7. Why do you think producers kept the price of going to the movies as low as possible during the Great Depression?

Vocabulary in context

D. Find a word or expression in the box with the same or similar meaning as the word or expression from the text.

> reduced   total number of people present   strong
> necessary   extremely important   very small
> cost of an entry ticket   unable to read or write
> grew a lot   art form   period   insist on

1. line 6: relevant ___ Nesesary
2. line 28: flourish ___ Grew lot   tant
3. line 40: admission ___ cost of ticket
4. line 44: stiff ___ Strong
5. line 44: paramount ___ Extremly
6. line 48: illiterate ___ Unable to read or write
7. line 56: medium ___ Art form
8. line 58: demand ___ INsist ON
9. line 63: age ___ Period
10. line 67: attendance ___ total number of people presen
11. line 70: dampen ___ Reduced or read
12. line 75: meager ___ Vert Small

Discussion

E. Why do you think people collect movie posters? In addition to posters, in what other ways are movies advertised? What do you think of these methods?

3 Grammar in Detail

Cause and effect

Practice

A. PAIR WORK Read the following sentences and determine what are the cause and the effect parts of the sentences. Write the parts under the appropriate headings.

Cause	Effect
The Great Train Robbery was exciting	Audiences wanted more movies like it

EXAMPLE:

> The Great Train Robbery *was so exciting that the audiences wanted more movies like it.*

1. There were so few jobs during the Great Depression that many people migrated to other parts of the country.
2. In *City Lights*, Chaplin was so funny that people could not stop laughing.
3. *Frankenstein* was such a terrifying movie that some people could not look at the screen.
4. After the widespread introduction of television, so few people went to the movies that the movie industry suffered serious financial problems.
5. Nowadays, some film stars make so much money that they are among the richest people in the world.
6. *The Great Train Robbery* was such a success that producers decided to make more movies like it.
7. Fascination with movie stars became so great that audience numbers increased a lot.
8. Technology for making movies developed so quickly that by the 1920s, sound was added to their production.

B. Read the statements in A again and sort them into the three categories below. Then write two more sentences of your own for each category.

so + adjective *or* adverb + *that* + effect

so + quantifying adjective + noun + *that* + effect

such + descriptive adjective + noun + *that* + effect

C. Express a cause-and-effect relationship by matching and combining the following pairs.

1. Those stars became so popular in Hollywood.
2. The moviegoers earned such low wages.
3. That movie had so many violent scenes.
4. Television was such a great success.
5. We have so little time these days.
6. Living in a quiet place is so important for us.
7. I've got so little work tonight.
8. Technology has advanced so much.

a. Going to the movies is impossible.
b. We don't miss movie theaters and malls.
c. I might go rent a video movie.
d. They were given the highest salaries.
e. We videotape our telephone conversations.
f. The movie industry suffered.
g. The movie theaters lowered the price of admission.
h. Some people left the theater.

D. Write the sentences below to emphasize cause and effect.

EXAMPLE:

> *I was so surprised to see my brother that I couldn't speak.* (normal)
> *Such was my surprise when I saw my brother that I couldn't speak.* (emphatic)
>   *or*
> *So surprised was I to see my brother after so many years that I couldn't speak.* (emphatic)

1. The desert was so hot that they couldn't walk any farther. (Use *hot or heat.*)
2. The wind was so strong that a lot of houses were destroyed. (Use *strong or strength.*)
3. The waterfall was so powerful that the tourists were amazed. (Use *powerful or power.*)
4. We were so tired that we went to bed at 7 p.m. (Use *tired or exhaustion.*)
5. The mountains were so high we could see for what seemed like hundreds of miles. (Use *high or height.*)
6. She was so angry with her employees that she fired them all. (Use *angry or anger.*)

Cause and effect

Such . . . that (normal)	Examples
With singular count nouns, use *such* + *a/n* + adjective + singular noun + *that . . .*	*It was such a good movie that the audience applauded at the end.*
With plural count nouns and singular non-count nouns, use *such* + adjective + noun + *that . . .*	*The actress had such beautiful eyes that audiences fell in love with her.* *That restaurant serves such delicious food that it's hard to get a table.*

Such . . . that (emphasis)	Examples
Use *such* with an abstract noun and without an adjective. Separate *such* from its noun and invert the verb.	*Such was his love for her that he forgave her everything.*

So . . . that (normal)	Examples
So + adjective or adverb + *that*	*This fad is so popular that everybody is doing it.* *The choir members worked so intensely last month that they are now exhausted.*
So much / little + (adjective) + non-count noun + *that . . .*	*There is so little (upbeat) entertainment in the country that I would get bored living there.* *There is so much (good) food in this city that I am sure to eat a lot while I'm here.*
So many / few + (adjective) + count noun	*I've got so few (real) friends here that I don't want to stay.* *There were so many (high) dunes in the desert that they got tired walking over them.*

So . . . that (emphatic)	Examples
Use with *so* + adjective + *that . . .* Keep the adjective together with *so* and invert the verb	*So tired were we that we went to bed at once.*
Note: In all cases *that* can be omitted	*This fad is so popular everybody is doing it.*

Test yourself

E. Combine the following sentences. Use the emphatic form where indicated *(E)*.

EXAMPLE: *So many people wanted to see the movie that they ran out of tickets.*

1. Crowds of people wanted to see the movie. They ran out of tickets.
2. They were extremely lonely in New York. They decided to return to California. (E)
3. There was an awful lot of action in that movie. I couldn't follow the story line.
4. That restaurant serves really good food. We should go there after the movie.
5. The whales' song was very musical. Scientists thought it was made by humans. (E)
6. The wind was incredibly strong. People could barely walk down the street. (E)
7. She dances beautifully. Everyone wants to dance with her.
8. The goalkeeper was unbelievably agile. He saved five goals. (E)

Speaking focus

Getting a more detailed explanation

Here are some questions you can use to ask someone to explain an opinion. Really? Why is that? Can you tell me a little more about that? Why do you say that?

Think about it

A. PAIR WORK What's the best movie you've seen recently? Tell your partner about it. Why did you like it? What's the worst movie you've ever seen? Practice using the expressions to ask your partner to explain.

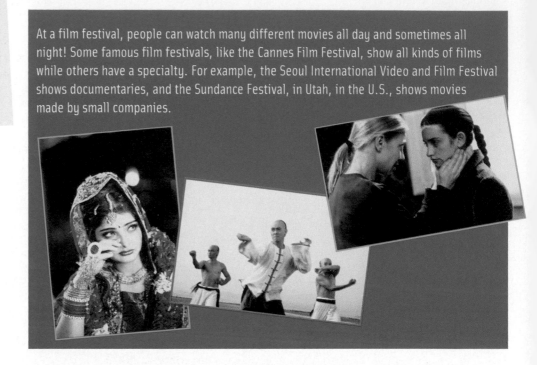

At a film festival, people can watch many different movies all day and sometimes all night! Some famous film festivals, like the Cannes Film Festival, show all kinds of films while others have a specialty. For example, the Seoul International Video and Film Festival shows documentaries, and the Sundance Festival, in Utah, in the U.S., shows movies made by small companies.

B. PAIR WORK You are members of a committee that is planning a film festival in your city. With your partner, choose movies for the following categories and compile lists of your selections.

> The three funniest movies ever made
> The three most exciting movies ever made
> The three scariest movies ever made
> The three most romantic movies ever made

C. GROUP WORK Now get together with another pair. Give your film festival a name and plan your schedule, with three different showings on Friday, Saturday, and Sunday. Choose from the movies you named in B and give reasons for your selections and for the order of the viewings.

D. Take turns sharing your film festival schedules with the class. Did anyone's choice of movies surprise you? Why?

A. Read the text and try to understand the **highlighted** words.

During the Second World War, in addition to **war movies, documentaries** once again became popular, as audiences **demanded** to know what was really happening in the **areas of conflict.** After the war, however, television became popular and the movie industry suffered a major **crisis.** Many stars, producers, directors, and **scriptwriters** lost their jobs. Gradually, the novelty with television wore off and the movies experienced a **revival** in the 1960s, thanks in part to the appearance of glamorous characters like James Bond in his **role** of **Secret Agent** 007. Other **spy** movies were also popular during the Cold War period. Then, in the late 1960s and early 1970s, movies such as *The Graduate,* where the **plot,** or **story line,** and the dialog, or **screenplay,** were just as important as the action, made a comeback. But **advances** in technology in the 1970s and 1980s changed the movies forever when **special effects** became the key to the success of **box office smashes.** Thus, **blockbusters** like *Star Wars, Superman,* and *Ghostbusters* introduced audiences to a genre of movie that continues to be a firm favorite today.

B. Work in pairs to find the answers.

1. Two terms that mean a very successful movie _____
2. Two words for a person who tries to discover the secrets of enemy governments _____
3. Two words for the story that a movie tells _____
4. The word for a movie that is about real life _____
5. The word for a movie that is about conflicts _____
6. A word with a similar meaning to *comeback* _____
7. The expression for places where people are fighting wars _____
8. A word similar in meaning to *emergency* _____
9. A word which means to ask for something very emphatically _____
10. A word with a similar meaning to *progress* _____
11. A word for the part an actor plays in a movie _____
12. An expression for sights and sounds in a movie which seem real but are not _____
13. A word for the people who write the dialog for a movie _____
14. Another word for the dialog in a movie _____

C. PAIR WORK Discuss a movie that you both have seen recently. Discuss which genre of movie it is and all the reasons why you liked or disliked this particular movie. What did you think of the actors, the screenplay, the plot, the special effects? Use headings like the ones below to prepare a short talk for the class about the movie.

Name of movie _____ Principal actors _____
Genre of movie _____ Special effects _____
Plot _____ Director _____
Reasons why we liked or disliked it _____

Listening strategy

Listening with a purpose

Before you listen, think about what you need the information for. This helps you to decide which information is important.

Before you listen

A. PAIR WORK Where do you get information about new movies? How do you decide which movies you want to see? Where can you find movie schedules?

B. You want to see a movie with a friend on Saturday. You will finish work at 8:30. Your friend must be home before 12:00 midnight. You call two movie theaters to listen to their recorded schedules. What information do you need to listen for?

First listening

C. Listen and write the names of the movies.

Avalon Theater

	Movie	Time
Cinema 1		
Cinema 2		
Cinema 3		

CineClub Theater

Theater 1		
Theater 2		
Theater 3		
Theater 4		

Second listening

D. Listen again. If there is a show time that you and your friend can attend, write it next to the name of the movie.

After listening

E. PAIR WORK Decide which movie you would like to see and why.

Test yourself

F. Read the question and think about the specific information you need to listen for. Then listen and answer the question.

At which branch of the bank can you get money on Saturday afternoon?
    a. at the Main Branch
    b. at the City Tower Branch
    c. at the Airport Branch
    d. at none of the branches

7 Writing

A movie review

Before you write

A. GROUP WORK In groups of four, discuss the following questions. How do you decide which movie you want to see or rent? Do you ask your friends for their opinions? Where can you find reviews of the latest movies? Do you ever read or listen to movie reviews?

B. In the same groups as in A, read the following movie reviews and answer these questions.

a. Which review is positive about *Blade II* and which is negative?

b. What is the source of these reviews and how do you know this?

c. What style are these reviews written in—formal or informal? How do you know?

Our Reviews

Blade II

Give me a break! by Peter

What can I say? I am at a loss for words to describe how truly awful this movie is. If you like brain dead, emotionless trash to flow over you for two hours, then maybe you'll enjoy this. This film reminded me of the sequel to Tarantino's <u>From Dusk Till Dawn</u> when a perfectly good thriller turned into a disaster, and you couldn't care less who died, as all the characters turned out to be totally horrible. If this is the best in action films, give me a good old weepy musical any day!
www.indetailmoviereviews.com

It only gets better! by Nuria

<u>Blade II</u> is a great film for sci-fi junkies, full of action right from the word "go." It's an exciting adrenaline ride from beginning to end. Wesley Snipes is superb in his role of vampire-hunter and the special effects make the first <u>Blade</u> movie look dull. They even made some of us scream! A brilliant way to forget about your problems—so, for my money, <u>Blade II</u> gets six stars out of five!

Write

C. Still in your group of four, choose a recent movie that you have all seen. Discuss your opinions of the movie. Then decide which two of you will write a positive review of the movie and which two will write a negative review. Remember that you are writing personal reviews for an Internet site, so the style can be quite informal.

A. GROUP WORK In groups of five or six, take turns miming the titles of famous movies that your teacher assigns to you. Play charades, dividing the class into two teams. A member of one team should mime a movie title for the other team, who must guess the movie within a set time period.

B. In new groups of four, try to agree who are the four most popular male and the four most popular female movie stars in your group. They can be dead or alive. Prepare to give reasons for your choices. Share your most popular movie stars with all your colleagues, and decide who are the four most popular male and female actors for the whole class.

C. CLASS TASK Do you have a movie industry in your country? If so, what are the names of some of the most famous directors, producers, and movie stars? What kinds of movies do they make? Do you like the movies produced in your country? Give reasons. If you do not have a movie industry, where are most of the movies that you watch made? Do you think foreign movies have any positive or negative effect on the culture of your country?

For more on movies, view the CNN video. Activities to accompany the video begin on page 143.

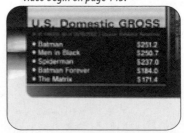

Review Your Grammar

A. Circle the verb form in parentheses that correctly completes each sentence.

1. If I were free to travel, I (would, can, would have) visit Hollywood.
2. I (would, will, could have) go there next year if I have the time.
3. Leo will come with me if he (was, is, has) the time.
4. Leo (might, may, can) have been an actor, if he hadn't been so shy.
5. If I (am, were, had been) Leo, I would have taken acting lessons.
6. He could have become a good actor if he (isn't, weren't, wouldn't have been) so shy.
7. I (go, will go, would go) to three movies this weekend if I have time.
8. If I (get, would get, got) tired of the movies, I would have to start reading books.

B. Complete each sentence with the correct passive form of the verb in parentheses.

1. (clean) _____ your teeth _____ by a dentist in the past six months?
2. (complete) _____ the work _____ in less than an hour?
3. (assist) _____ the dentist _____ by a hygienist?
4. (tell) _____ you _____ to brush every day?
5. (pay) _____ the bill _____ by your insurance company?
6. (ask) _____ you _____ to make another appointment?

High Challenge

C. Write the letter of the underlined word or phrase in each sentence that is incorrect.

1. The marathon <u>was won</u> by a young woman <u>from</u> Africa who <u>had trained</u>
                A   B   C
   <u>by</u> an excellent coach. _____
   D
2. She had <u>so</u> strong legs <u>that</u> she <u>could run</u> for hours without <u>getting</u> tired. _____
           A   B   C   D
3. She was <u>such a</u> <u>fast</u> runner <u>that</u> the race <u>completed</u> in record time. _____
            A   B   C   D
4. If the weather <u>had been</u> hotter, the runners probably <u>would not run</u> so
                 A   B
   <u>fast</u> and the race <u>would have taken</u> longer. _____
    C   D
5. There were <u>such</u> many people at the race <u>that</u> my friends <u>were</u> <u>lost</u> for
             A   B   C D
   hours afterwards. _____

FYI

Some international tests include grammar items that consist of sentences containing four underlined words or phrases. You are asked to pick out the incorrect word or phrase in each sentence. Read the sentence four times, substituting one of the underlined words or phrases with a blank in your mind. Decide how you would fill that blank. Compare your answer with the underlined word or phrase.

Review Your Vocabulary

A. Using one word from each box, complete each sentence with a compound adjective.

broad flat high
good brown fat

cheeked natured eyed
footed shouldered spirited

1. Most of the dancers were very excitable and _____.
2. Because the dance teacher was so _____, she got along well with everyone.
3. Alvin was so _____ that there was no chance he would ever learn to dance.
4. Rob was _____ and didn't have any trouble lifting his partner above his head when he had to.
5. The lead dancer was _____ and also had long, blond hair.
6. The dancers were all very thin. Not one of them was _____ and heavy.

B. Circle the word that doesn't belong.

1. thigh   abdomen   hips   steel
2. plot   story line   span   screenplay
3. waterfall   temple   palace   museum
4. eyes   lips   waist   cheek
5. fjord   cliff   mountain   spy
6. salsa   comedy   fantasy   biography

C. Unscramble the words below. Then write the words in front of the correct definitions.

beweroy	kelan	dahasem	nemadd	issoa	esir

1. _____ It's how you might feel when you fail.
2. _____ It is a way of asking for something.
3. _____ It's above the eye.
4. _____ It's the opposite of *fall*.
5. _____ It is found in a desert.
6. _____ It's above the foot.

Review Your Speaking

Fluency

A. Look at the photograph and describe what is happening. Then discuss the questions.

1. Do you know any landmarks in Los Angeles? Can you describe one of these landmarks?
2. Would you like to visit Los Angeles? Why or why not?
3. If you could visit any big city in the world, which one would you choose? Why?

B. Tell a partner or a small group about a movie you enjoyed. Answer any questions they may have.

Here are some things you might include:
- Name the movie
- Tell when and where you saw it
- Describe the type of movie it is
- Tell who the stars are
- Describe the best scene

F•A•Q   How can I improve my pronunciation?

Teachers do not generally have time to help students individually improve their pronunciation, but there are many helpful books with tapes or CDs that you could use to work on your pronunciation by yourself. When you are working alone, you need to listen carefully to the tape or CD and try to imitate the sounds, stress, and intonation that you hear. You can also make a list of words that are difficult for you to pronounce and ask someone with good pronunciation to record these words for you so that you can practice them until you improve.

Review Your Listening

Listening 1

A. You are going to hear a conversation about a TV program. Listen and check the type of program the conversation is about.

1. Game show
2. Soap opera
3. Travel program
4. Sports program

B. Read through these new words and their possible meanings. Then listen again and decide what each word probably means.

1. A **travelogue** is
   a. a story about a trip   **b.** a special prize   **c.** a kind of car
   d. a sad movie
2. An **expedition** is
   a. a way to send things   **b.** an exciting story   **c.** a difficult trip
   d. a test
3. **Remote** means
   a. expensive   **b.** very modern   **c.** boring   **d.** far away

Listening 2

C. Now you'll hear a conversation about another TV program. Check the word that describes what Rosa is watching.

1. Opera _____
2. Dance _____
3. Theatre _____
4. News _____

D. Read through these questions and think about the kind of information you need to listen for. Is it general or specific? Then listen again and answer the questions.

1. Rosa is studying very hard.	T	F
2. Rosa often watches this kind of program.	T	F
3. Dave thinks Rosa shouldn't watch TV so much.	T	F
4. The program is from another country.	T	F
5. Rosa is worried about her exam.	T	F

Risk

Communication

Making deductions; giving advice

Discussing risks and justifying choices

Narrating facts about conflicts or peace processes

Grammar

Modal verbs with present, past, and perfect infinitive

Vocabulary

Occupations: risks and benefits

Peace, war, and conflict

Idioms using conflict terms

Skills

Reading informal job descriptions

Listening and note taking

Writing a personal letter expressing sympathy

1 Warm Up

A. PAIR WORK Describe the pictures. Where do you think the people are? What do you think they are doing? What are their occupations? What do all of these occupations have in common? Would you like to have any of these occupations? Why or why not?

B. Combine words from the box on the left with words from the box on the right to form as many occupations as you can.

EXAMPLE: *a systems engineer*

systems fire war dance soccer mountain gold petroleum police bus TV dog space computer movie travel secret Formula One	programmer miner agent guide engineer fighter producer driver journalist officer instructor trainer player climber

C. Share the occupations you have found with the class and list all the occupations on the board. Use a scale from 1 to 5 to show the level of risk in each occupation: 5 = highest risk, 1 = least risk. Discuss why you think some of the occupations have more risk than others.

Reading strategy

Distinguishing between facts and opinions

Look out for those words and phrases that express objective facts and those more emotive words and phrases that express subjective opinions.

Before you read

A. In groups, brainstorm to determine all the facts you know about astronauts, Formula One drivers, war journalists, and firefighters. Try to answer questions like these below in your groups.

Who was the first astronaut to travel into space? Which country was the first to land a man on the moon? What recent developments have there been in space travel?

Who are some of the world's most famous Formula One drivers? Where do some of the most famous Formula One races take place?

In which parts of the world might war journalists work today? What are some of the risks they run?

In which parts of the world are forest or bush fires very common? In addition to helping extinguish fires, what else do firefighters do?

First reading

B. Skim the two readings and check (✓) the occupations that are represented.

war journalist _____   Formula One driver _____
firefighter _____   astronaut _____

Facing Danger on the Job

I. Each mission° is meticulously planned, so on the whole, I am not too **scared** when the time comes for us to leave. Once you are up there, you experience certain **inconveniences** in your daily routine—little things that
5 are so easy in normal living conditions are **a whole new ballgame** up there. For example, food is as weightless as you are, so you have to catch it in your mouth. And I can tell you, that is exactly what you learn to do—otherwise, you would **starve.** The food is not that bad, in fact. Most
10 of it comes in cans or pouches, which we heat. Some is **dehydrated,** so we just add hot water and eat it. There is a shuttle° that delivers the food on a weekly basis, and small amounts of fresh fruit and vegetables are allowed. When we get to eat the fresh stuff, boy do we feel good!
15   It's not the food which is the biggest problem though; it's the **isolation.** Knowing that you are so far away from your family can **tear you apart,** and if you've got young kids, it can be pretty tough. That's when thinking about

20 the risk of the return trip can become unbearable. Fortunately, we are allowed one video phone call to our families a week and we can e-mail them on a daily basis.
    When we are not working, there is a very intensive physical exercise program that we have to follow. It has
25 been scientifically proven that significant degradation° of the body occurs during these missions—they negatively affect the bones, internal organs, and cardiovascular system, and the longer we stay up there, the more significant the changes. All of which I find
30 worrying, I have to admit, but the good news is that exercise reduces these changes, and a lot of them can be reversed° when we get back.
    II. I think it must have been the most terrifying experience in my life. A week earlier, I had secretly
35 entered the area where the rebels° were operating. The national government had recently **banned** any communication with them, so this meant that I was not allowed to interview them.

It was, however, not the rebels I was interested in; it
40 was the ordinary people who lived in rebel-held
territory. I had no political agenda—just my agenda as a
professional observer. I felt I should let the world know
about the terrible humanitarian crisis in the area. The
people in this **zone** were starving; food was not being
45 distributed; there were no medicines or clean drinking
water and no fuel for cars or lighting. It was this
unnecessary suffering that I had reported and now I was
going home.

After some local guides and I had been walking for
50 days through thick jungle and muddy rivers, we had, at
long last, reached the border between rebel and
government territory. All I had to do was cross that
border—just fifty yards from where we were hiding. It
should have been so easy! But luck was not on my side.

55 My guides had been informed that it would not be
militarized, but in fact, there were dozens of soldiers°
near the crossing, and it was late at night and very
dark. How could I convince them that I was not a rebel
but simply a woman just trying to do her job?
60 Something caught their attention and one of the
soldiers fired°. I was hit. But I **survived,** and even
though I lost the hearing in my left ear, I am
determined to get back to work as soon as possible.

mission = journey	crisis = emergency
shuttle = a vehicle that travels	soldier = a person who fights for
regularly between two places	his or her country
degradation = loss of strength	fire = use a gun
reverse = change back	
rebel = person who resists the	
government	

Second reading

C. Read closely and find these facts.

1. Why is eating in space difficult?
2. Where do astronauts get their food?
3. What is the biggest problem astronauts face while in space?
4. Why do they have a daily exercise program while in space?
5. What did the war journalist want to report from this specific conflict area?
6. What kind of areas had she and her guides been walking in for days?
7. Why was she terrified when she got to the crossing?
8. What happened to her at the crossing?

Think about it

1. Why do you think the astronauts enjoy the fresh food so much?
2. Why do you think astronauts with young children find their jobs particularly stressful?
3. Why do you think the ordinary people in the rebel-held territory did not have the basic necessities of life?
4. Why did night make the journalist's crossing especially difficult?

Vocabulary in context

D. Find words or expressions in this list with similar meanings to the words or expressions used in the text.

> controlled by soldiers   area   frightened   die of hunger   without water   to live in spite of a serious problem
> not allowed   difficulties   land   loneliness   completely different   to make you very sad

1. Line 2: scared _Frightened_
2. Line 4: inconveniences _difficulties_
3. Line 5: a whole new ball game _completely different_
4. Line 9: starve _die of hunger_
5. Line 11: dehydrated _without water_
6. Line 16: isolation _Loneliness_
7. Line 17: tear you apart _to make you very sad_
8. Line 36: banned _Not allowed_ soldiers
9. Line 40: territory _Land_
10. Line 43: zone _area_
11. Line 56: militarized _Controlled by soldiers_
12. Line 61: survived _to live in spite of serious problems_

Discussion

E. Imagine you had to choose one of the two occupations in the text. Which one would you choose and why? Why would you not want to do the other job?

3 Grammar in Detail

Modals with present, past and perfect infinitive

Practice

A. PAIR WORK Match the statements on the left with the concepts on the right.

1. In space, you have to follow a daily exercise program.
2. Being far away from your family can tear you apart.
3. Governments should help the innocent people who live in conflict zones.
4. "We may get to the border before night falls," the guide told the journalist.
5. "May I take pictures of ordinary people when I go to rebel-held territory?" the journalist asked.
6. "You must do what I say," said the soldier to the journalist.
7. "I can't hear a thing you're saying," said the journalist to her guide after she was injured.
8. "You should go to a hospital immediately," a doctor told the injured woman.

a. strong advice.
b. moral obligation.
c. ability.
d. permission.
e. theoretical possibility.
f. strong obligation (rules).
g. possibility.
h. necessity.

B. Complete the text below with one of these modals.

> may (possibility)   can (ability)
> must (strong obligation)
> should (strong advice)
> can (theoretical possibility)

If you are planning a vacation trip to space in the future, you **(1)** _____ make sure you are in very good physical and emotional shape before the trip. Space travel **(2)** _____ have serious negative effects on the human body, especially on muscles and bones. Once in space, you **(3)** _____ do exactly what the space team tells you to do. Sometimes, there **(4)** _____ be an emergency on board, but don't panic, as today space teams **(5)** _____ solve almost all their problems either by fixing things themselves or by contacting earth for remote support.

C. Match the *past tense structures* on the left with the concepts on the right.

1. It was so dark they *couldn't* see a thing.
2. The journalist *was not allowed* to enter the conflict zone.
3. After many difficulties, she *managed to* get to a hospital.
4. She *had to* travel for hundreds of miles in an old four-wheel drive.
5. They *had to* give the soldiers all their papers and pictures.

a. necessity
 _d_
b. strong obligation
 _c_
c. permission
 _e_
d. general ability
 _a_
e. one specific past ability
 _____

D. Complete the text with the correct form of the past tense structures from C.

Last year, I wanted to go trekking in the Gobi Desert, but my doctor **(1)** _____ me to because I wasn't in very good physical shape, so I **(2)** _____ change my plans. At the very last minute, I **(3)** _____ get a place on a safari trip to Kenya, and it proved an excellent choice. Every day, we traveled by four-wheel drive to the safari parks where we **(4)** _____ see all the wild animals and take as many pictures as we wanted to. I would have liked to walk around the parks but we **(5)** _____ stay in our vehicle all the time, as the animals can become quite aggressive when people start walking around taking pictures of them.

E. Match the past perfect statements on the left with the concepts on the right.

1. It *must have been* the worst experience of her life.
2. Someone in the group *may have made* a noise that attracted the soldiers' attention.
3. The journalists *shouldn't have entered* the rebel-held zone in the first place.
4. She *could have found* interesting stories in less dangerous areas.

a. a possibility that did not happen
b. a logical deduction about something that happened
c. criticism or regret about something that happened
d. a possible explanation for something that happened

F. Complete the dialog with the correct form (negative or positive) of these modals.

> may have   must have   should have   could have

A: _____ (you) _____ gotten here a little earlier? We're too late for the show.

B: So, sorry! My watch _____ stopped. I thought I was early.

A: It stopped last week, too. You _____ bought another one.

B: I know, but I've been so busy. Come on, let's go and ask. The show _____ started yet, and they might let us go in.

Modals with present, past, and perfect infinitive

Present tense meanings of modal verbs	Past tense meanings of modal verbs
can: (1) ability, (2) theoretical possibility *may:* (1) permission, (2) possibility *have to:* necessity *must:* strong obligation *should:* (1) advice, (2) moral obligation	*could:* general past ability (applies to more than one occasion) *allow (to):* permission *manage / be able (to):* be able to do something on one specific past occasion *had to:* (1) strong obligation (2) necessity

Past perfect constructions with modal verbs

must have + **past participle:** a logical deduction about something that has happened
could have + **past participle:** a possibility that did not happen
should have + **past participle:** a criticism, regret, or accusation about something that has happened
may have + **past participle:** a possible explanation for something that has happened

Note: Some modal verbs can be used in various ways to express different ideas. This unit deals with some of the uses and meanings of some common modal verbs.

Test yourself

G. Choose the correct form and tense (positive or negative) of a modal verb and of the verb in parentheses to complete these dialogs.

1. "Are we staying in again tonight? I think we **(a)** _____ (try) to get out more." "Yeah, I know. We **(b)** _____ (go) to the movies, but it's too late now. **(c)** _____ you (leave) work a little earlier?" "Well, I'll try. We **(d)** _____ (be) so busy next week, so maybe we can go out then."

2. "Hi, how was your trip?" "Awesome! It **(a)** _____ (be) the best trip I've ever had. You **(b)** _____ (come) with me." "I know, but this year I **(c)** _____ (take) my vacation in July. We were so busy while you were away. I **(d)** _____ (work) till 10 p.m. every night. I'm going to look for another job. There are so many other things I **(e)** _____ (do) instead of this!"

Speaking focus

Showing that you are paying attention

You can show the other person that you're paying attention to them by using expressions like these. These are especially useful when you are talking on the phone.

Uh-huh.   Mm-hm.   Really?
I see.   Oh?

A. PAIR WORK What makes a good job? A bad job? Do you think most people's ideas about this are similar or different? Use the expressions above when listening to your partner.

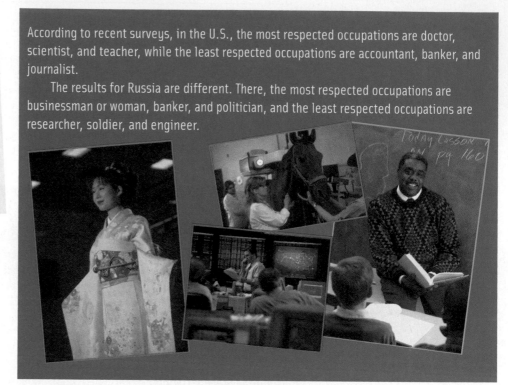

According to recent surveys, in the U.S., the most respected occupations are doctor, scientist, and teacher, while the least respected occupations are accountant, banker, and journalist.

The results for Russia are different. There, the most respected occupations are businessman or woman, banker, and politician, and the least respected occupations are researcher, soldier, and engineer.

B. GROUP WORK Work with another pair. Look at the list below and discuss the meaning of each item and which jobs can offer these things. Make notes about why each point is important or not important for you.

excitement	status
job security	balance of work and family life
salary and benefits	independence
variety	creativity
helping other people	(your own idea)

C. Look at your notes. Imagine you want to find the perfect job. Circle the three things on the list that are the most important for you.

D. GROUP WORK Take turns telling your group about the three things that are important for you. On the basis of people's priorities, suggest possible jobs for each group member.

E. CLASS TASK Discuss your classmates' suggestions. Did you like any of them? Who came up with the most interesting ideas?

5 Vocabulary in Detail

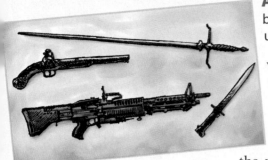

A. Read the text and look at the pictures. Then complete the exercise below using words and phrases in bold type from the text. Be sure to use the correct form of the word or words.

Wars start when **troops** from the **army,** the **navy,** or the **air force** of two countries or groups of people **fight against** one another. In a war, each **side** uses a variety of **weapons.** When human beings first began to **wage wars,** the weapons they used were quite primitive: **swords** and **spears,** for example. Then **firearms,** such as **pistols** and **machine guns,** were invented, and these innovations transformed the way in which wars were fought. With the development and use of **bombs,** especially the **atom bomb** at the end of the Second World War, nations from **all over the world** got together to establish international **peace-keeping organizations,** like the United Nations, to try to prevent future wars. Although **conflicts** still occur in many parts of the world, most countries prefer to **resolve their differences** through **peace processes,** as they are aware that the use of modern methods for fighting wars, that is, **nuclear, chemical,** and **biological weapons,** could lead to the **destruction** of humankind.

1. Another word for war is _____.
2. An atom bomb is an example of a _____.
3. A machine gun is an example of _____.
4. The opposite of war is _____.
5. The United Nations is an example of a _____.
6. Another word for large numbers of soldiers is _____.
7. Two examples of modern weapons are _____ and _____.
8. A word for a country that is taking part in a war is _____.
9. Another way of saying "fight a war" is _____.
10. In order to avoid war, nations need to talk with each other and _____.

B. PAIR WORK Choose one of the words or expressions in A, for example, war, peace process, chemical weapons. Working together, prepare a few sentences about this particular topic in which you use other words from A.

C. Match the idiomatic expressions on the left with the explanations on the right.

1. He didn't *set the world on fire* as a politician, but he made some contributions to peace processes.
2. When I arrived, they were *firing* insults at one another.
3. She *is a real ball of fire!* I can't keep up with her.
4. They *are all fired up* about the project.
5. Apparently, he's *fighting a losing battle* with Alzheimer's.
6. He *put up a good fight* but died as a result of his injuries.
7. James *got fired* because his work wasn't good enough.
8. In the course of a peace process, *fighting fire with fire* is not an option.

a. be a very energetic person
b. be dying of
c. be very enthusiastic
d. exchange very quickly
e. not be very successful
f. use the same methods as your enemies
g. try hard to get better
h. lost one's job

Listening strategy

Taking notes

As you listen, try taking notes to help you remember the most important information. Good notes are short. They contain only the most important words—not whole sentences.

Before you listen

A. PAIR WORK Have you ever seen a circus performance? Did you enjoy it? Why or why not? What kinds of acts can you see at a circus? What kinds of animals are there?

First listening

B. You are going to hear an interview with Andrew Colmer, a tiger trainer for a famous circus. Listen and take notes about his tigers.

Second listening

C. Listen again, and take notes about the day Andrew describes.

Tigers

Size: _____
Food: _____
Sleep habits: _____
Likes: _____

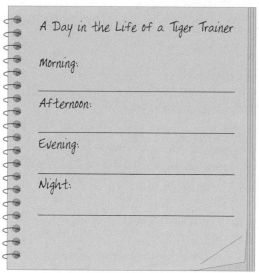

A Day in the Life of a Tiger Trainer

Morning: _____

Afternoon: _____

Evening: _____

Night: _____

After listening

D. How does Andrew feel about his work? Do you think he's afraid of the tigers? Why or why not? Why do people like to watch animals at the circus? Can you think of any other kinds of entertainment that involve risk?

Test yourself

E. Listen and take notes about a very different kind of risky job: a bicycle messenger. Remember, good notes contain only the most important words.

Bicycle Messengers

Work: _____
Pay: _____
Equipment: _____

A personal letter expressing sympathy

Before you write

A. GROUP WORK In groups of four, discuss the questions below.

1. If you have a friend who has a serious problem—for example he or she is extremely ill, or has just experienced the death of a close relative, or has survived a terrifying experience such as a natural disaster—why might you decide to write a personal letter to that friend instead of calling or e-mailing?

2. What things would you try to put in your letter to help your friend?

B. Still in the same groups, read the letter and the envelope and answer the questions.

1. Why is James writing to Elizabeth?
2. Where exactly is Elizabeth at the moment?
3. How can you tell that Elizabeth was seriously injured?
4. How does James express sympathy in this letter?

Ms. E. Howard
St. John's Hospital, Ward 10
130 W. 72nd St.
New York, NY 10249

15th May

Dear Elizabeth,

I was really sorry to hear about your accident. It must have been a terrible shock for you to discover that you'll have to spend so long in the hospital. But I'm sure that you're receiving excellent care and that you'll make a steady recovery.

Guess what! I have to make a trip to New York next week, so I'll stop by and see you. I've read a couple of really good books recently—one is a travel journal by this guy who spent two months in the Gobi Desert. It's excellent and just the kind of thing I know you'd enjoy, so I'll bring it with me when I come. And let me know if there's anything else you'd like me to bring you. How about some of that chocolate ice cream that you like so much?

Thinking about you,

James

Write

C. In your groups, imagine you have a friend with a serious problem that is causing him or her a lot of suffering. It does not have to be an illness or accident. Write a two-paragraph letter to your friend, but first decide the kind of things you are going to say or propose in your letter to help your friend.

D. Exchange letters with another group in the class and comment on the contents of the other group's letter.

A. GROUP WORK Play a game of "What's my Line?" Decide on a real or imaginary occupation you would like to have. For example, you could be a superhero such as Spiderman. Join up with another group and take turns guessing what the occupation is. Ask only *yes/no* questions and try to guess what the occupation is after ten questions.

B. PAIR WORK Play a game of dangerous occupations—"Don't do it!" Work in pairs and list all the dangerous occupations that people in your country actually do. Then choose one and decide all the reasons why you want to have this occupation even though you know it is dangerous. Be prepared to argue against the reasons people might use to persuade you against it. Join another pair with a different occupation from yours and take turns trying to persuade the other pair against their chosen occupation and defending your choice.

C. CLASS TASK Do you know anyone whose father or mother has a dangerous occupation? How does that person feel about his or her parent's job? Discuss whether you think people with children should accept or continue in dangerous occupations. Give reasons for your opinions.

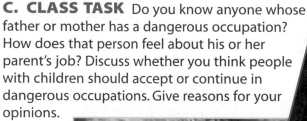

For more on risky activities, view the CNN video. Activities to accompany the video begin on page 144.

Friends

1 Warm Up

A. Describe these pictures.

• Do you find any of these friendships unusual?

• If so, why?

• How important are friends in your country?

• Is it easy for people from different ethnic, social and economic backgrounds or from different generations to make friends?

• Why or why not?

> to feel down   to be depressed   to feel loved and understood   to have a serious problem   to feel secure   to feel like a failure   to be in a state of shock   to feel thankful for   to be frightened   to feel relieved   to be heart broken   to feel lost and lonely   to feel comforted   to be excited

B. PAIR WORK Decide which column the expressions above belong in.

When we most need friends	How we feel when friends help us

C. Use suitable expressions from B to talk about an occasion when a friend helped you a lot.

EXAMPLE: *I felt depressed when my boyfriend and I broke up, but my best friend really took care of me. She came over to see me most evenings for the first few weeks and even made my favorite meal for me.*

Before you read

A. GROUP WORK Discuss the following statements. Give reasons why you agree or disagree with them.

1. A true friend should have the same opinion as you about everything.

2. A false friend is someone who tells your secrets to others.

3. A true friend will love you in spite of your faults.

4. A true friend will understand when problems get you down.

5. A false friend is someone who reminds you that you must learn to help yourself.

6. A true friend will listen to you when you have a problem.

7. A true friend will solve all your problems for you.

8. A false friend is someone who wants you to change and be exactly like him or her.

First reading

B. Skim the three poems that follow and identify the one in which the writer:

(a) reminds us that we must first be our own best friend before we look for friendship in others.

(b) expresses the different roles of a friend.

(c) suggests that friendship is a major source of happiness.

1. Everyone Needs Someone

People need people and friends need friends
And we all need love for a full life depends
Not on **vast** riches or great acclaim°,
Not on success or on worldly fame,
But just in knowing that someone cares
And holds us close in their thoughts and prayers°
For only the knowledge that we're understood
Makes everyday living feel wonderfully good,
And we rob ourselves of life's greatest need
When we "lock up° our hearts" and fail to **heed**
The **outstretched** hand reaching to find
A **kindred** spirit whose heart and mind
Are lonely and **longing** to somehow share
Our joys and **sorrow** and to make us aware
That life's completeness and richness depends
On the things we share with our loved ones
And friends.

Helen Steiner Rice

2. My Friendship

My Friend
Has a shoulder to lend.
My Ally
Will wipe the tears when I cry.
My Chum
Laughs with me, even when I'm dumb.
My Advocate
Is someone who will never quit.
My Patron
Will never look at me and shun.
My Supporter
Won't care if I'm shorter.
My Comrade
Will help when I'm sad.
My Friend
Will be with me to the end.

Emily Ryon

3. The Guy in the Glass

When you get what you want in your **struggle** for pelf°,
And the world makes you King for a day,
Then go to the mirror° and look at yourself,
And see what that guy has to say.
For it isn't your Father, or Mother, or Wife,
Who judgement° upon you must pass.
The feller° whose **verdict** counts most in your life
Is the guy staring back from the glass.
He's the feller to please, **never mind** all the rest,
For he's with you clear up to the end,
And you've passed your most dangerous, difficult test
If the guy in the glass is your friend.
You may be like Jack Horner° and "chisel a plum°,"
And think you're a wonderful guy,
But the man in the glass says you're only **a bum**
If you can't look him straight in the eye.
You can fool the whole world down the pathway of years,
And **get pats on the back** as you pass,
But your final reward will be heartaches and tears
If you've **cheated** the guy in the glass.

Peter Dale Wimbrow, ©1934 Dale Wimbrow

```
acclaim  =  public admiration
prayer  =  the act of talking to your God
lock up  =  close with a key
pelf  =  an informal word for money (very uncommon)
mirror  =  glass in which you can see yourself
feller  =  very informal word for guy
judgement  =  decision in a court of law
Jack Horner  =  character in a children's poem
chisel a plum  =  be very lucky (very uncommon)
```

Second reading

C. Read the poems and find the information.

Poem 1

1. What two things are much less important than friends?
2. What are some of the benefits of true friendship?
3. What is the main objective of true friendship?
4. What kind of person should a friend be?
5. What happens if people reject an offer of friendship?

Poem 2

6. What do you think "has a shoulder to lend" means?
7. What kind of things has this friend done to help the writer?
8. What is the difference between to laugh "with" someone and to laugh "at" someone?
9. How does the writer express the idea that this friendship will last?

Poem 3

10. Who is the guy in the glass?
11. Whose opinion of you should be most important to you in life?
12. Why is this person's opinion so important?
13. What does the mirror or glass represent?
14. How will you feel at the end of your life if you have not been honest with yourself?

Think about it

Give a definition of friendship you think all three authors would agree with.

Vocabulary in context

D. Find in the poems a word or expression with the same or similar meaning as these.

> **FYI** Judgement can also be spelled *judgment*.

1. unhappiness _____
2. "pay attention to" _____
3. make a great effort _____
4. great or very large _____
5. to fool: _____
6. forget about _____
7. great desire for _____
8. a useless person _____
9. judgement _____
10. are congratulated _____
11. similar _____
12. extended _____

Discussion

E. GROUP WORK Discuss which of these poems you like most. Why? Which ideas in the poems do you identify strongly with and which do you find difficult to identify with?

3 Grammar in Detail

3. Grammar in detail
The zero / habitual conditional; review of all conditionals

Practice

A. PAIR WORK Match the first part of the sentence on the left with the second part on the right.

1. If I didn't have so many good friends,
2. If he had listened to her friends,
3. If you were more open to friendship,
4. If she hadn't had her Internet friend,
5. If they had been true friends,
6. If I go abroad to work,
7. If he joined a choir or a salsa club,
8. If you come to live here with us,

a. he would find it easier to make friends.
b. I will have to make new friends.
c. you will find it easy to make friends.
d. you would be a happier person.
e. I would find life very difficult.
f. she'd have had no one to help her.
g. this quarrel would never have happened.
h. they would still be married.

B. Work alone and complete these statements with true information about your past and present habits. Note that in all these statements you can use *when,* or *whenever* instead of *if.*

1. If I had a problem as a small child, I_____
2. If I feel lonely and depressed, I _____
3. If my friends give me good advice, I _____
4. If I don't have a lot of work on the weekends, I _____
5. If I found my schoolwork too difficult, I_____
6. If our parents had visitors when we were children, we_____

Interact

C. PAIR WORK Ask your partner about his or her past and present habits and make a note of what he or she tells you.

EXAMPLES:
> *1. What did you do whenever you had a problem as a small child?*
> *Whenever I had a problem as a small child, I asked my grandfather for help.*
> *2. What do you do whenever you feel lonely and depressed?*
> *As a matter of fact, I never feel lonely or depressed.*

D. Use your notes in C to tell the class what you have learned about your partner.

EXAMPLES: *Whenever Jorge had a problem as a small child, he asked his grandfather for help.*

116   In Detail 1

The zero / habitual conditional; review of all conditionals

Type of conditional sentence	Notes
Habitual activity	
If I am happy, I share my happiness with a friend.	Both verbs are in the simple present.
If I had a problem as a child, I told my grandmother.	Both verbs are in the simple past.
Scientific fact or universal truth	
If there are a lot of cars in a city, pollution gets worse.	Both verbs are in the simple present.
If seawater evaporates, it rises.	Both verbs are in the simple present.
Real past affects future	
If they've practiced, they will play well today.	The verb in the *if* clause is in the present perfect or present perfect
If she's been working hard, she will go to bed early.	continuous, and the verb in the main clause is in the future tense.
Unreal present affects past	
If they weren't so skillful, they wouldn't have won.	The verb in the *if* clause is in the simple past, and the verb in the main clause is in the past conditional: *would/n't have* + pp.
Unreal past affects present	
If she hadn't gotten to a hospital, she would be dead.	The verb in the if clause is in the past perfect, and the verb in the main clause is in the conditional: would + simple or progressive infinitive.

Don't forget: With habitual actions, scientific fact, or eternal truths, *when* or *whenever* can replace if.

E. Match the beginnings of the sentences on the left with the endings on the right.

1. If the Gobi Desert weren't so vast,
2. If that team had a better manager,
3. If you've been walking in the desert all day,
4. If they have scored by half time,
5. If we had crossed the river by boat,

a. we will be so happy.
b. we would be in bed by now.
c. we would have seen all of it.
d. you'll get tired.
e. they would have been the winners today.

Test yourself

F. Use a check (✓) to indicate if the following conditionals are grammatically correct. Write an *X* if the sentence is not correct, and rewrite it.

1. If the temperature of water drops to 0° C / 32° F, the water freezes. _____
2. If I am feeling fed up, I went downtown. _____
3. If people travel to the Gobi Desert, it is because they love adventure. _____
4. If you've been working hard, you relaxed. _____
5. If she hadn't gone on vacation into space, she wouldn't feel so weak now. _____
6. If he weren't so selfish, she hadn't divorced him. _____
7. If the soldiers had seen those journalists, they would be dead now. _____
8. If they have reached the top of the mountain by now, they will be so happy. _____

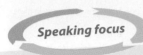

Speaking focus

Introducing a difficult topic

If we want to talk about a sensitive or difficult subject, we can introduce it with expressions like these below.

Well, you know, …
I hate to say it, but, …
I've been thinking, …
I have to tell you, …

Think about it

A. PAIR WORK What kinds of problems do friends sometimes have? If you have a problem with a friend, how do you try to solve it?

Below are some proverbs from different cultures about friends.
   The best mirror is a friend's eye. (Irish)
   Books and friends should be few and good. (Spanish)
   It is easier to visit friends than to live with them. (Chinese)
   Make new friends but keep the old, one is silver and the other gold. (English)

B. GROUP WORK Your teacher will assign one of these situations about a group of friends. With your group members, choose a role. Think about different ways to solve the problem, and try to use expressions for introducing a difficult topic. Make short notes. Then practice your conversation with your group.

Situation 1:
A: You borrowed some money from your friends B and C. Decide what you needed it for. Now you're having problems and you can't pay it back. **B:** You think that A sometimes spends money for useless things and should be more careful. **C:** You think that B worries about money too much.

Situation 2:
A: You have a new boyfriend or girlfriend and you're very happy because you spend so much time with him or her. **B:** You feel sad because you don't see A very often now. **C:** You think that A's boyfriend or girlfriend doesn't like you. Think of a possible reason.

Situation 3:
A. You have joined an organization. Decide what kind of organization it is. You are spending a lot of time working with the group. You really want your friends B and C to join. **B:** You disagree with the ideas of this organization and you don't want to join. **C:** You think that A is working too hard and needs to relax and have fun with you.

Situation 4:
A: You're upset because B said something that made you feel bad. Decide what it was that B said. **B:** You didn't mean anything bad. You don't understand why A is upset. **C:** You want A and B to be good friends again.

When you're ready, take turns performing your role plays for the class.

C. Discuss the role plays with the class. Who had some interesting ideas? Who found good solutions to these problems?

5 Vocabulary in Detail

A. Read the following text and try to understand the **highlighted** words.

I consider myself pretty lucky because I have lots of friends. Then there's Mobbo. (His real name's Kevin.) I've known him since we were like four years old and he's my **best friend.** I know that he really likes this girl in our class called Mariana. I think there's something going on between them but he says that they're "**just good friends.**" Yeah, right!

Sometimes it takes time to **make friends** with someone. There's this one guy, Carl, in my class. He was new last year. For months, I didn't really take any notice of him. The truth is, I thought he was kind of weird, you know? Then I discovered that we actually **have a lot in common.** Now we're real good **buddies.**

Sometimes you have a good friend and he or she is also friends with someone else, and you get to meet this person and you like them too, so then you have a **mutual friend.**

Of course, there are some people—**fair-weather friends,** my grandma calls them—who *say* that they're your friend, but if you're in trouble and you need like a favor or something, they suddenly act like they don't know you. I hate that! My grandma also says you need to know the difference between friends and acquaintances.

For me, a true friend is someone who is **loyal.** That's really important. I remember this one girl called Lisa. I thought she was my friend and I **confided in** her about all sorts of personal stuff. Later I found out that she had told people all sorts of terrible things about me! Can you believe that?

I have this one friend—his name is Lars. I think he's from Sweden or somewhere. Anyway, among my group of friends, people are pretty **demonstrative.** People quite often greet each other with a kiss or a hug. **To our great amusement,** Lars always blushes and looks embarrassed when people greet him like that, especially if someone **gives him a hug.**

> F Y I
>
> A **friend** is someone you know well.
> An **acquaintance** is a person you have met and know slightly but not well, for example, someone who is in the same exercise class as you.

B. PAIR WORK Work with a partner and find bold-faced words or expressions in A that match these descriptions.

1. we find something very funny
2. put your arms around someone
3. to form a new friendship
4. to tell your secrets to
5. a special friend that you like the most
6. someone who is a friend of yours and also a friend of mine
7. two people like or believe similar things
8. a good friend
9. someone who is always true to you
10. someone who expresses his or her feelings openly
11. a friend who runs away once his or her friends have a problem
12. two people, one male and one female, are only friends and not boyfriend and girlfriend

C. Work alone and prepare two short talks, one about a really good experience with a friend and the other about a bad experience with a friend. Use words and expressions from A.

D. Underline the correct meaning of the idioms in the sentences below.

1. A true friend never *turns his or her back on* you.
2. A true friend will never *stab you in the back.*
3. A true friend will *back you all the way.*
4. If you *have your back to the wall,* a true friend will help you.
5. You will always be glad to *see the back of* a bad friend.

(a) never goes away **(b)** never rejects you
(a) kill you **(b)** do something very disloyal
(a) support you in all circumstances **(b)** go on long journeys with you
(a) have a serious problem **(b)** are standing up
(a) see him or her leave forever **(b)** see him or her with no shirt or blouse

Listening strategy

Listening for the main points and examples

Identify each main point and the examples of that point to help you understand the most important information in a speech or presentation.

Before you listen

A. PAIR WORK You are going to listen to a talk entitled *How to Be a Better Friend*. What ideas do you have about this topic? What advice would you give to someone who wants to become a better friend?

First listening

B. Listen to the talk and fill in the four main points and the conclusion.

How to Be a Better Friend

1. _____ wisely.
   Advice: _____
   _____

2. Make _____.
   Advice: _____
   _____

3. _____ things.
   Advice: _____
   _____

4. _____!
   Advice: _____
   _____

Conclusion: _____
Proverb: _____

Second listening

C. Listen again and take notes (in short phrases) on the specific advice that Dr. Maynard gives.

After listening

D. PAIR WORK Look at your partner's notes and add more information. Do you agree with Dr. Maynard's ideas? Is Dr. Maynard's advice appropriate in your country?

Test yourself

E. Listen to another short talk and answer this question. What is the main idea of this talk?

1. Writing to a "key pal" is a good way to improve your English.
2. The Internet has changed many aspects of modern education.
3. Language students often have problems understanding native speakers.
4. You should always try to write about subjects that you are interested in.

7 Writing

A Haiku poem

Before you write

A. GROUP WORK Brainstorm to come up with all the words you know in English that express feelings and emotions. Then discuss the ways in which you like to communicate different feelings or emotions. For example, when you are happy, do you sing or dance? When you are sad, do you talk to a friend or do you go to a movie to try and forget your problem? Recently, many psychologists have recommended that people should write to help express their emotions. Does anyone in your group write poetry to express his or her feelings?

B. In the same groups, answer the following questions:

1. What do you notice about the three poems below?
2. Where do you think the author of each poem comes from and why?
3. Which of the poems is about (a) nature; (b) the importance of friends and family; (c) unhappiness?
4. What are some of the things all three poems have in common?

Haiku

Family and friends,
Are near and dear for ever
Like quiet forest
—*Bonnie Best*

This then is morning
Have you no comfort for me,
Cold-coloured flowers?
—*Masako Takahashi*

Water jar cracks:
I lie awake
This frosty night
—*Basho*

C. Now read the text below and answer the following questions.

1. What is the main characteristic of a Haiku poem?
2. In which country has Haiku been popular for hundreds of years?
3. Why do you think people all over the world are trying to write Haiku today?

Haiku is a form of short poem, which the Japanese have practiced for centuries, and that millions of Japanese still enjoy writing today. A haiku has three lines: the first line is five syllables, the second line is seven syllables and the third line is five syllables. Haiku is a contemplative poem which attempts to convey a vivid impression in very few words. Often, Haiku reflects on nature and relates the external world (nature) to the author's internal world (feelings). In the last ten years or so, haiku has become popular in many countries, including the United States.

Write

D. GROUP WORK In your groups, choose a suitable theme for a haiku poem. Write the poem. Then get together with another group of students and read and comment on their poem. Make any changes you feel necessary and then share the final version of your poem with the rest of the class.

A. Work alone and use the outline below to make notes about the best friend you have ever had.

> **Name:**
> **Nationality:**
> **Place and occasion you first met:**
> **Length of your friendship:**
> **Reasons why you are such good friends:**
> **Qualities in your friend you particularly admire:**
> **Example of something your friend did for you that was very special:**

Copy the outline again and get together with another student. Interview one another about the best friend you have ever had and complete the second outline. Tell the class about your partner's best friend.

B. Here are some difficult situations you might find yourself in with a friend or a group of friends. In groups, discuss what you would do if you found yourself in these or similar situations. If you have had a similar experience in your own life, tell your group about it.

1. A very good friend of yours has a boy- or girlfriend who is not liked by your friend's parents. Your friend tells you that his or her parents have said to stop seeing this person. You also do not like this because you know that he or she is not loyal to your friend. Your friend confides in you that he or she is going to keep on seeing this person in secret.

2. You and your best friend have been inseparable for years. Your friend has only just learned to drive. He or she invites you to go out for a drive to a famous landmark. On the way there, you feel that your friend is driving much too fast and dangerously and you are really frightened. You simply cannot face the journey back home.

3. Your best friend has been unemployed for the past six months and has spent a lot of time on the Internet looking for a job and "chatting" to Internet friends. There is one Internet friend with whom he or she has become very close. This Internet friend lives thousands of miles from your town or city. Your friend confides in you that he or she has been invited to visit this Internet friend and is going to accept the invitation.

For more on friends, view the CNN video. Activities to accompany the video begin on page 145.

C. CLASS TASK As a class discuss this statement: I could live without my family but not without my friends. Discuss whether you agree or disagree with this statement and compare the importance of family in your culture with the importance of friends.

Television

1 Warm Up

A. Look at the pictures and discuss the kinds of television programs they represent. Which kinds of programs do you watch? Which kinds of programs would you never watch? Give your reasons. ....

B. Match the TV programs with the descriptions.

quiz show	comedy show
sitcom	documentary
weather forecast	drama series
talk show	travel program

1. a program that gives factual information about a person or a subject such as science, nature, history, or social issues

2. a program in which people answer questions and the winner or winners win prizes such as money, cars, or vacation trips

3. a program in which people narrate their experiences as they visit and explore interesting places in the world

4. a program in which there is a host who invites guests to talk about their lives; often there is an audience in the TV studio, and members of the audience also participate in the program

5. a program in which people tell jokes

6. a weekly series about the dramatic events in certain institutions, for example, hospitals, schools, police stations

7. a continuing series in which viewers follow the sometimes strange and usually amusing events in the lives of the same group of people

8. a short program in which you find out what kind of clothes you need to wear that day

C. CLASS TASK Discuss which you think are the best TV programs in your country.

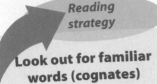

Reading strategy

Look out for familiar words (cognates)

Many languages are related, so you may find words that are the same or similar to words in your own language. These words are called cognates. Use them to understand a reading text.

Before you read

A. Discuss these questions in small groups.

How important is TV to you and your family? How many hours a day is the TV on in your home? Is it on during mealtimes? Do you think this is a good or a bad thing? Where do you usually look for information about TV program schedules?

First reading

B. Scan this section of a newspaper to find the following information.

1. On which channel can you watch a good movie tonight?
2. At what time can you see a program about movie stars?
3. About which continent has the series *Travel Journal* been reporting?
4. Which countries are playing in the friendly, international soccer matches?
5. Which new book is top of the list for English language teaching?

Our Choice of Evening Viewing

Babe: Pig in the City **7:00 – 8:30 Film Channel 5** A delightful sequel to the hit *Babe,* this movie begins where *Babe* **left off.** It has a good story line and lots of talking animals, and it's an excellent excuse for families
5 **to unite** around the television.

Global Issues **8:30 – 9:30 NBC 1** This week's *Global Issues* takes us to South Africa to observe the impressive efforts of a group of women in a South African township° who have taken on the job of building
10 their own houses. Tired of waiting for the government to provide them with proper houses, these women got bank loans so that they could take classes in construction—making bricks°, mixing cement. Just two years later, they have finished building their own comfortable homes and
15 repaid their loans. What's more, they are now teaching unemployed men how to make bricks and mix cement! Why this series was scheduled on a Saturday evening **beats** me, especially with the competition from *Life's a Laugh* on NBC 2. A Monday or Tuesday evening would
20 have been a more appropriate time to schedule such **thought-provoking** material. I doubt whether this particular program in the series will get the audience° it deserves.

Hollywood Couples **9:30 – 10:30 NBC 1** Even
25 though most of us claim not to be **remotely** interested in the lives of Hollywood couples, let's face it, we love these shows. This weekly show, in which famous Hollywood couples talk about their **stormy** relationships, has a **phenomenally** large audience. Who will the couple
30 be tonight? As usual, their identity is revealed° only at

the start of the program, but last week, host Burt Fox **hinted** that
35 there might be a big age difference between this week's spouses. Well . . . your
40 guess is as good as mine, but for my money° it's Michael Douglas and Catherine
45 Zeta-Jones.

Travel Journal **9: 30 – 10:30 NBC 2** If you can resist *Hollywood Couples* on NBC 1, you should definitely tune into this last **episode** of Jan Simpson's

Asian adventures. Having **trekked** through some of the
50 most difficult parts of the Gobi desert and climbed to the
summit° of one of the highest peaks in the Himalayas,
she completes her three-month Asian experience with a
relaxing but nevertheless **informative** week in
Cambodia's awesome° temple city of Angkor Wat, one of
55 the great wonders of the East. Beautifully filmed and
sensitively reported, this is **stiff** competition for
Hollywood Couples.

World Soccer Roundup **11:00 – 11:30 NBC 1** This
late-night review of soccer highlights from around the
60 world focuses tonight on a series of friendly,
international matches being played in the run up to the
World Cup. These matches are sure to produce lots of
action and we hope, a few goals. Can the U.S. make
history and beat Brazil, or will **the latter's** years of
65 experience help resist the pressure from **the former's**
young but talented team, unbeaten in its last seven
matches? As for Japan vs. Thailand and Turkey vs.
Korea, these games are so evenly matched that it is hard
to predict the results. Both Thailand and Turkey are
70 suffering injury troubles, which puts them at a
disadvantage. Thailand's flamboyant and skillful
striker, Anand Leekpai, has a broken foot, while Hakan
Buruk, Turkey's formidable° goalkeeper, is out with a
dislocated shoulder.

75 *Global Language* **10:30 – 11:00 NBC 2** A
fascinating report on the status of English as a global
language with reviews of the latest books for teaching
it. At the top of the list, is **In Detail 2** so check it out!

township = a town where formerly only black people lived in South Africa	reveal = provide information that has been secret
brick = a block of hard clay used as building material	for my money = in my opinion
audience = all the people who watch a TV program	summit = the highest part of a mountain
	awesome = inspiring admiration
	formidable = extremely strong or powerful

Second reading

C. Read to find these specific details.

1. What movie is *Babe: Pig in the City* the sequel to?

2. How did the women in the South African township get the money to pay for their training in construction?

3. When do we find out who the Hollywood couple for each program is?

4. How long has Jan Simpson been traveling?

5. What kind of team is the U.S. fielding at the moment?

Think about it

1. Why do you think a lot of people might not want to watch serious programs like *Global Issues* on a Saturday night?

2. Why do you think so many people watch *Hollywood Couples*?

3. Why do you think Jan Simpson is probably feeling very tired?

4. Why might both Turkey and Thailand lose their matches?

5. Why do you think *Global Language* provides information about the best books for teaching English?

Vocabulary in context

D. Find a word or expression in the boldface text with a similar meaning to those below.

1. amaze
2. get together
3. an event in a series of events
4. stopped
5. suggest in an indirect way
6. very emotional
7. providing a lot of facts
8. the first of two things or people already mentioned
9. serious or major
10. exceptionally
11. traveled or walked with difficulty
12. inspires you to think
13. a little
14. the second of two things or people already mentioned

Discussion

E. With the class, discuss which three programs in the TV program review you would watch on a Saturday evening and why. Why wouldn't you watch the others? Would you watch them another evening? Why or why not?

3 Grammar in Detail

Noun clause: subject, object, complement

Practice

A. PAIR WORK Read these sentences and underline the subjects and the objects or complements. Then indicate whether they are nouns, noun clauses, pronouns, or adjectives.

EXAMPLE: <u>Why this program was scheduled on a Saturday evening</u> (S noun clause) beats <u>me.</u> (O pronoun)

1. What you said about that program shocked us all. *s* _____ *o* _____

2. What he did to his best friend was unforgivable. *s* _____ *o* _____

3. He did something unforgivable to his best friend. *s* _____ *o* _____

4. I understand how much you are suffering. *s* _____ *o* _____

5. I understand your suffering. *s* _____ *o* _____

6. We doubt whether our team will win the match. *s* _____ *o* _____

7. We doubt our team's ability to win the match. *s* _____ *o* _____

8. Whether the program will be a success is the question. *s* _____ *o* _____

9. The critics doubt the success of this program. *s* _____ *o* _____

10. They claim that it is the worst program in years. *s* _____ *o* _____

B. Match the first part of the statements on the left with the second part on the right.

1. What I saw in that documentary	a. was a great disappointment.
2. We do not know	b. (that) they have good houses.
3. Why he did that to his friend	c. if they will win.
4. Some people do not believe	d. shocked me.
5. The women know	e. what I said.
6. That they lost the match	f. what movie critics write.
7. I doubt	g. is still a mystery to us all.
8. He didn't like	h. where she went.

Interact

C. Work with a partner and decide if the prepositions in the following pairs of sentences are followed by a noun (N) or a noun clause (NC).

EXAMPLE:
I am interested in what you have to say. (NC)
I am interested in your opinion. (N)

1. (a) My friends asked my parents about what I was doing. _____
   (b) My friends asked my parents about my work. _____

2. (a) The audience was not convinced by what that politician had to say. _____
   (b) The audience was not convinced by that politician. _____

3. (a) Whether our team wins the match or not will depend on luck. _____
   (b) Whether our team wins the match or not will depend on how lucky we are today. _____

4. (a) Think about your reasons for doing that. _____
   (b) Think about why you did that. _____

5. (a) That teacher is totally obsessed with his own ideas. _____
   (b) That teacher is totally obsessed with what he thinks and believes. _____

D. Work alone and complete the statements with true information about yourself. Then work in pairs and use the information to tell your partner things about yourself.

EXAMPLES:
(1) I'm going to play table tennis this afternoon. It's great exercise. That's what matters. I don't care whether I win or not.
(2) I bought a new digital camera yesterday. I had no idea how much it would cost, but in fact, it wasn't all that expensive.

1. I don't care whether *I win or not.*

2. I had no idea how much *it would cost.*

3. I am interested in _____

4. I am sure that _____

5. I doubt whether _____

6. I can't understand why _____

7. I am worried about what _____

8. I am not convinced by _____

Noun clause: subject, object, complement

Rules	Examples
1. If the noun clause is the object of the verb, and it is introduced by the connector *that*, *that* can be omitted.	1. *Movie critics often believe (that) only famous actors can be successful.*
2. *That* cannot be omitted if the noun clause is the subject of the sentence.	2. *That I am happy despite my problems says a lot about my friends.*
3. *Wh-* connectors can never be omitted, whether they introduce the subject, direct object, or the complement.	3. (a) *I don't believe what you say.* (b) *Why he did that is still a mystery.* (c) *This is what I believe.*
4. The noun clause can replace the noun as the object of a preposition.	4. (a) *Your health depends a lot on what you eat.* (b) *We were shocked by how quickly their friendship ended.*

Test yourself

E. Identify the noun clauses in these statements. Indicate whether they are the subject *(S)*, the complement *(C)*, the object of a verb *(OV)*, or the object of a preposition *(OP)*.

1. Whether Kidman will act in that movie is still the most important question. _____
2. What that soldier did was very courageous. _____
3. Do you know where astronauts get their food from? _____
4. I'm worried about my friend. Do you think that she will recover from her injuries? _____
5. That actor is very competent. He is always so sure of what he does and says. _____
6. I can't understand why my friend has not called me. _____

4 Speaking

Speaking focus

Giving specific examples

You can help a listener understand your ideas better by giving specific examples. Here are some expressions you can use.

For instance ... for example ... An example of this is ... Let me give you an example ...

Think about it

A. PAIR WORK How many hours of TV do you watch a week? What kinds of programs do you like? Did you watch TV much when you were a child? Did your parents put any restrictions on the types of programs you could watch? Use the expressions above to give examples.

> **Position:** The effects of TV on people are mostly _____.
> **Reason 1:** _____
> **Explanation:** _____
> **Reason 2:** _____
> **Explanation:** _____
> **Reason 3:** _____
> **Explanation:** _____

B. GROUP WORK With your classmates, plan and carry out a mini-debate on this topic: *The Effects of TV on People Are Mostly Positive / Negative.* Your teacher will assign you a position. This position might not be your real opinion! With your team members, discuss ideas and fill in the chart. Be sure to give examples.

C. GROUP WORK Now join with a team that discussed the opposite position. Tell them your reasons and explanations. Listen to the other team and take notes on their reasons.

D. GROUP WORK Go back to your original team. Talk about the other team's reasons and think of arguments against them. Make notes. Then meet again with the other team and take turns giving your arguments against the other side.

E. What are some of the principal positive and negative effects of TV on people?

A recent survey found that the average American child watches three to four hours of TV each day. By age sixty-five, the average American has spent nine years of his or her life watching TV!

A. PAIR WORK Read the definitions in sentences 1 to 10 below and find in the list on the right, a word or expression that matches each definition.

1. a compound noun for all the different ways in which people receive information in the world today

2. an adjective to describe a TV program, a film, or a newspaper article that tries to tell the truth without expressing an opinion

3. what some governments do to newspapers, books, or films, if they disapprove of certain parts or aspects of them

   a. subjective
   b. sensationalism
   c. indoctrinate
   d. counterproductive
   e. moral standards
   f. mass media
   g. corrupting
   h. objective
   i. censor
   j. a commercial

4. an adjective to describe a piece of writing, a film, or a TV program that presents only the producer's or the writer's personal point of view

5. what a piece of writing, a movie, or a TV program does if it teaches readers and viewers that certain opinions and ideas are the only correct ones

6. an adjective to describe the kind of influence violent programs and movies might have on children and young people

7. a compound noun for the basic beliefs and principles that help people to live honest lives

8. a word to describe a short advertisement on TV or radio.

9. an adjective that shows that something might have the opposite effect of what is intended

10. a noun to describe a way of reporting news that appeals only to the emotions and prejudices of readers or viewers and not to their intellects

B. Now decide if the words in A are positive or negative.

C. Work with the class and put the words in the box into the correct column in the chart.

(to) indoctrinate   a censor
corrupt   informative
(to) corrupt   censorship
commercial   corrupting
indoctrination   (to) censor
counter-productive
(to) inform   a commercial
thought-provoking

Verb	Noun	Adjective for state	Adjective for effect

D. GROUP WORK In groups of four, choose either a TV program that all of you watch regularly or a newspaper that you read regularly and prepare a short talk about it. Use words from C and organize your talk under the following headings:

Name of program	Type of program	Purpose of program	Evaluation / opinion of program

Before you listen

A. PAIR WORK What kinds of TV programs have a lot of violence in them? Who likes to watch these kinds of programs? Do you watch them? Why or why not?

First listening

B. You are going to hear two speakers, Dr. Murphy and Ms. Parker, talk on the subject of TV violence. What is the main idea of their talks? Select your answer from the options below and write it.

Dr. Murphy says
Ms. Parker says

. . . parents should control their children's TV viewing.
. . . violence on TV makes the world more violent.
. . . networks make exciting TV shows because they're popular.
. . . violent TV programs are a problem only for children.
. . . the government should not make laws about TV programs.

Second listening

C. Listen again. Who would agree with these statements? Write *M* for Dr. Murphy, *P* for Ms. Parker, or *X* for neither after each statement.

1. In real life, people sometimes copy things they see on TV. _____
2. TV programs are less violent now than in the past. _____
3. Watching violence on TV can sometimes be good for people. _____
4. Children don't understand the difference between TV and real life. _____
5. TV makes us more violent in real life. _____
6. Networks produce violent programs because people want them. _____
7. Programs about real life are not very interesting. _____
8. All TV programs should be suitable for children. _____

After listening

D. PAIR WORK Which of the above statements do you agree with? Explain your reasons.

Test yourself

E. Look at the questions below. Do you need to listen for general or specific information? Then listen to the talk and answer the question.

What does the professor mainly talk about?
a. how television affects our lives
b. the invention of the first television
c. the history of TV programs
d. how a television works

Listening strategy

Deciding whether the information you need is general or specific

Before you listen, think about what kind of information you need to find. Is it the general idea? Or is it specific information?

7 Writing

TV reviews

Before you write

A. GROUP WORK On a piece of paper, write the names of two TV programs you really enjoy and two you dislike. Then mingle with your classmates until you find at least two, but not more than three, other people with similar tastes to yours.

B. Working in the same groups, first talk about why you like and dislike the programs you have listed. Then complete the following notes for each program.

	Two programs we like	Two programs we dislike
Name		
Schedule		
Type		
Purpose		
Reasons for your opinion		
Suggestions		

Write

C. Imagine that you are TV critics and that you have been asked to write the reviews for *This Evening's Viewing*. Use your notes to write four short reviews. Use a similar format to the one in the reading text *Our Choice of Evening Viewing*.

D. Join with another group. Exchange your reviews and make comments on the other group's reviews. Are they well written? Are they convincing? Give your reasons.

A. PAIR WORK Work alone and prepare to describe your favorite TV commercial and the commercial you dislike most. Join with another student and take turns describing your favorite commercial and the one you dislike most, without naming the products being adverted. Try to guess which commercials your classmate is describing. After you have guessed all four commercials, discuss the reasons why you like and dislike the commercials you chose.

B. PAIR WORK As a whole class, decide on a recent movie or a TV program about which people have very strong and opposing opinions. Get into pairs and decide who is going to be the censor and who is going to be a member of the public who does not want to censor the program or movie.

Censors: Work alone and take a few minutes to list all the reasons you want to censor the program or movie and which specific parts you would censor.	**Noncensors:** Take a few minutes to list all the reasons you think the program or movie should not be censored. Prepare to respond to the objections the censors might make about the program or movie.

C. CLASS TASK Discuss with the class all the changes and improvements that you would like to see in the TV networks of your country. Identify the programs you feel are most in need of change and reform, and suggest ways to improve them or suggest ideas for alternative programs.

D. CLASS TASK Evaluate *In Detail Student Book 1*. First work alone and take a few minutes to skim through all the *In Detail Book 1* units. Think about which units you found most entertaining, most thought-provoking, most informative, most unusual, easiest, most demanding. Then share your opinions with the class and give reasons for them. Vote for your favorite units and record the results on the board.

For more on television, view the CNN video. Activities to accompany the video begin on page 146.

Review Unit 4

Review Your Grammar

A. Complete the second sentence of each pair so that it means the same thing as the first sentence.

may have   may   should have   had to   allow manage

Use a modal from the box.

1. It's okay if you want to turn off the TV.
   _____ if you want.
2. When I was a child I couldn't watch TV after 9:00 at night.
   _____ when I was young.
3. I was required to be in bed by 9:00.
   _____ by 9:00.
4. Were you able to find *TV Guide* magazine?
   _____ to find *TV Guide* magazine?
5. Maybe I pushed it under the couch when I was cleaning up.
   _____ when I was cleaning up.
6. It would have been a good idea for me to be more careful.
   _____ more careful.

B. Complete each sentence with the correct conditional form. Use the verb in parentheses.

1. (be) If I _____ not busy, I get nervous.
2. (have) When I was young, I watched TV whenever I _____ any free time.
3. (watch) If you _____ a lot of TV, your mind gets lazy.
4. (not join) If I _____ the swim team, I would still be watching TV all the time.
5. (be) If I had started swimming sooner, I _____ a better swimmer.
6. (win) If the coach has been telling me the truth, I _____ all my races at Friday's meet.

C. Combine each pair of sentences using a noun clause.

1. I know something. You don't know what I know. (that)
2. Laura said something. I couldn't believe her. (what)

3. I can't tell you what it is. It really bothers me. (that)
4. I don't understand. Why did she tell me the secret? (why)
5. I've been worried. I hope I don't tell someone I shouldn't tell. (that)
6. Why do people talk about their secrets? It's a mystery to me. (why)

High Challenge

D. Choose the best completion for each sentence.

1. I don't understand _____ my friends call me before 9:00 on Saturday morning.
   a. if
   b. that
   c. why
   d. what
2. If I am sleeping soundly, their calls _____ me up.
   a. are waking
   b. woke
   c. have woke
   d. wake
3. I think they _____ wait until at least 10:00 to call.
   a. should
   b. must
   c. may
   d. have to
4. I don't believe _____ they need to talk to me that early in the morning.
   a. what
   b. that
   c. why
   d. how
5. If I _____ them so much, I would really yell at them.
   a. wouldn't love
   b. loved
   c. hadn't loved
   d. didn't love

> **FYI**
> In some standardized examinations, the grammar test includes items that ask you to choose the correct words to complete a sentence. Look at all the choices carefully before you choose your answer. The incorrect answers, which are called distractors, are chosen to look as if they could be correct, so that the correct answer does not appear too obvious. If you choose your answer too quickly, you may make a mistake.

Review Unit 4

Review Your Vocabulary

A. Match each word with the correct definition.

___ **1.** dehydrated   **a.** related to

___ **2.** vast   **b.** afraid

___ **3.** kindred   **c.** not allowed

___ **4.** scared   **d.** without water

___ **5.** banned   **e.** showing strong emotions

___ **6.** demonstrative   **f.** very wide or large

B. Use words and phrases from the box to complete the conversation.

> formidable   losing battle   soccer player   state of shock   salaries   all fired up
> phenomenally   ball of fire

Pablo: You know what I'd like to be—a world famous **(1)** _____.
Kim: Well, you'd have to be **(2)** _____ good to become world famous.
Pablo: I know. But I'm a real **(3)** _____. Maybe I have a chance.
Kim: I think you'd be fighting a **(4)** _____.
Pablo: But I hear that soccer players make great **(5)** _____.
Kim: I'm sure they do. But you're up against **(6)** _____ competition.
Pablo: I know. And I would be in a **(7)** _____ if I made the national team.
Kim: But you're still going to try, aren't you?
Pablo: You bet! I'm **(8)** _____.
Kim: Well, best of luck to you.

C. Check the best response.

1. Does Lila work with computers?
___ Yes, she's really loyal.
___ Yes, she's a systems engineer.

2. Do you think we can resolve our differences?
___ No, I think we'll end up waging war.
___ Yes, I feel broken-hearted.

3. The boss really liked your work.
___ I know. She gave me a pat on the back.
___ I know. I had my back to the wall.

4. Do you know when the new boss is coming in?
___ Yes, he will depart on the 15th.
___ Yes, my old boss confided in me.

5. Will you miss your old boss?
___ Yes, it beats me.
___ Yes, it tears me apart that she's leaving.

6. Did you read the company newsletter this month?
___ Yes, it contains some thought-provoking articles.
___ Yes, it has a lot in common.

Review Your Speaking

Fluency

A. Look at the photograph and discuss with a partner or a small group which people in the photograph you think are friends. Give reasons.

B. Read about the three types of friendship. Then tell a partner about some of your friends that fall into each category and explain why.

1. Equal friends—both people are loyal and affectionate and generous to each other; both people share equally in giving and receiving the benefits of friendship

2. Receptive friends—one partner does more giving and the other does more taking, but both people get something good out of the relationship

EXAMPLES: *teacher and student, doctor and patient*

3. Casual friends—there is no strong loyalty or trust; the relationship is not intense, but there is warm feeling between the two people

EXAMPLE: *neighbors, coworkers, classmates*

F•A•Q There are so many different accents in English—how will I ever learn to understand them all?

Take heart, you are not alone! Even people whose first language is English sometimes have difficulty understanding other English speakers whose accents are different from their own. If you don't understand what someone has just said, you should try to let that person know in a polite way. You can say, "I'm sorry, I didn't quite get what you said" or "I'm having a bit of trouble following you." Another way to handle this situation is to try to rephrase what you believe the person may have said. To check with the person you can say, "If I understand you, what you are saying is . . ." or " I'm not totally sure, but did you ask me . . .?"

Review Your Listening

Listening 1

A. A stuntman (or stuntwoman) replaces the actors in dangerous scenes of movies. You are going to listen to an interview with Alan Morgan, a movie stuntman. After you listen, you will write a short paragraph about "Alan Morgan's Dangerous Career." Which of these kinds of information are useful for writing your paragraph? Underline them. Then listen to the first part and circle the ones that are in the interview.

> his wife's name   his daily routine   how he learned to do stunts   his favorite food
> his work week   his hobbies

B. Listen again and take notes to help you write your paragraph. Remember, good notes are short and contain only the important words.

_____

_____

_____

_____

_____

_____

_____

Listening 2

C. Before listening to the second part of the interview, read this list and underline the information that would be useful for writing your paragraph. Then listen and circle the ones that are in the interview.

> types of stunts he does   where he lives   accidents   his salary   music he enjoys
> what he likes about his work

D. Listen to the second part again and take notes for your paragraph.

_____

_____

_____

_____

_____

_____

_____

Unit 1: Tuxedo Trends

Before viewing

A. PAIR WORK In your country, what kind of clothes do people wear for formal occasions like ceremonies or parties? If you were invited to a very formal party, what would you wear? Would you enjoy wearing those clothes? Why or why not?

> nostalgia   polyester
> costume   pastel (color)

B. You are going to watch a video about formal clothes for men. Check the meaning of the words in the box.

First viewing

C. Read the questions, then watch and take notes. Answer the questions after you watch.

1. What is a tuxedo?
2. When were these tuxedoes made?
3. Which colors are the most popular?
4. What colors do men prefer? What about women?
5. Why do men wear tuxedoes like these?

Second viewing

D. Watch again, listening for these slang words. Then match them to their meanings.

1. hip _____
2. retro _____
3. threads _____
4. knock-offs _____

a. clothes
b. fashionable
c. copies or imitations
d. from an earlier time

After viewing

E. Talk about these questions.

1. Would people in your country ever wear clothes like these? Would you ever wear them?
2. Are there any fashions from the past that are popular now? Why do you think people like to wear fashions from the past?
3. Think about fashions this year. Which ones will people wear thirty years from now?

Unit 2: India Wedding Day

Before viewing

A. PAIR WORK What do you know about India and its people, their religions, their languages, their culture?

B. You are going to watch a video about a wedding ceremony in India. What do you think you will see?

meld   tradition
ancestors   kinship

C. Check the meaning of the words in the box.

First viewing

D. Read the questions, then watch and take notes. Answer the questions after you watch.

1. How long do weddings usually last?
2. How long did this ceremony last?
3. How did Richa meet her husband?
4. Who is joined together in an Indian wedding, besides the bride and groom?
5. Why is this time of year popular for weddings? (two reasons)

Second viewing

E. Watch again, and find the answers to these questions.

1. In Richa's opinion, what is important for a good marriage?
2. What evidence do Indians have that their system works well?

After viewing

F. Talk about these questions.

1. What surprised you in the video? Is anything similar to your country?
2. Are there marriages like Richa's in your country? Do you think they can be successful?
3. In your opinion, is keeping tradition more important or less important today? Why?

Unit 3: Dayjams

Before viewing

A. PAIR WORK Do you play a musical instrument? How did you learn? Do you know anyone who plays in a band or other musical group? How did they learn to play together? What's the best way to learn to play music in a group?

B. You are going to watch a video about a music camp for children. What do you think you will see in the video?

chord   frustrated
tune (n)   beats (n)

C. Check the meaning of the words in the box.

First viewing

D. Read the questions, then watch and take notes. Answer the questions after you watch.

1. What is Dayjams, in your own words?
2. How long do the kids stay at the camp?
3. How old is Max? How long has he been playing the drums?
4. Which instrument does Jordan play?

Second viewing

E. Watch again and find this information:

1. the goal of the program at Dayjams
2. what Max says he learned at Dayjams
3. what the teacher says the kids learn

After viewing

F. Talk about these questions.

1. How does their music sound? Do you think they are learning anything?
2. Do you think they will be successful musicians in the future?
3. Do you think Dayjams is a good idea? Why or why not?

Unit 4: World Cup Culture

Before viewing

A. PAIR WORK Where was the World Cup held in 2002? Why was this unusual? Do you remember anything that happened then?

B. Watch the video with the sound turned off. Which countries do you think these people are from?

First viewing

C. Watch the video and write down five countries/nationalities that are mentioned.

1. _____   2. _____   3. _____
4. _____   5. _____

Second viewing

D. Read through these statements. Then watch again, and answer True or False. If the sentence is false, change it to make it true.

1. Soccer fans didn't have much opportunity to learn about Japanese culture.
   True   False
2. The World Cup stadiums were in the biggest Japanese cities.
   True   False
3. Japanese people came to support foreign teams.
   True   False
4. A Japanese player played in an African league.
   True   False
5. The fans thought the World Cup was very well organized.
   True   False
6. Some local people were afraid before the foreign visitors came.
   True   False

After viewing

E. Talk about these questions.

1. How do sports fans benefit from attending an international tournament?
2. Does the host country also benefit from having an international tournament?
3. Has your country ever hosted an international sports event? Was it a good experience, or a bad experience? Do you want your country to do this in the future?

Unit 5: Ecotourism in Brazil

Before viewing

A. Do you know anything about ecotourism? What do you think it means?

B. PAIR WORK Where can travelers see unusual and interesting environments in the world? In your country? Which of these places would you like to visit? Why?

C. Check the meaning of the words in the box.

preservation	biodiversity	rainforest	ecosystem	monitoring

First viewing

D. Read the questions, then watch and take notes.

1. Where did the Reynolds family go in Brazil?
2. Why did they go there?
3. What did they think about their experience?
4. Where do ecotourists go?

Second viewing

E. Watch again, and fill in this information.

What are the good effects of ecotourism on Brazil?
1.
2.

What are the bad effects?
1.
2.

What might control these bad effects?
1.
2.

After viewing

F. Talk about these questions.

1. Would you like to go on a vacation like this in the Amazon rainforest? Why or why not?

2. Where could ecotourists go in your country?

3. Is tourism mostly good or bad for your country? Are there any places in your country where tourism has caused problems?

Unit 6: Cell Phone Driving

Before viewing

A. PAIR WORK In your country, do people talk on their cell phones while driving? What do you think about this—is it okay, or is it a problem? Are there any laws about using cell phones in your country?

B. Check the meaning of the words in the box.

dial (v)	legislation	ban	evidence

First viewing

C. Watch the video and match the sentence parts.

Nicky Taylor	got in an accident while calling a radio station
John Korzain	thinks cell phones make cars safer
Jackie Robinson	wants a law to control using cell phones in cars
The American Automobile Association	was in a car accident caused by a cell phone

Second viewing

D. Watch again and fill in the spaces.

1. Even the head of the National Highway Safety Administration says _____ cell phones in cars is premature, though forty states are considering legislation and at least ten localities have passed _____. The cellular industry says common sense can't be legislated, and the American Automobile Association points out that by facilitating the prompt _____ of accidents, cell phones have actually _____ lives . . .

2. A couple of recent polls highlight a dilemma. In one, _____% said they would like to see a _____ on using cell phones while driving. But when another poll asked, "Would you obey such a ban?" _____% said _____.

After viewing

E. Talk about these questions.

1. What is the evidence for allowing people to use their cell phones in cars? What is the evidence against it?

2. Would people in your country obey a ban on talking on the phone in cars?

Unit 7: Irish Dancing

Before viewing

A. What do you know about Ireland? Have you ever seen traditional Irish dancing? Heard Irish music?

B. PAIR WORK Have you ever done folk dancing of any kind? Do you enjoy watching it? Why or why not? Do you think it's easy to learn?

C. Check the meaning of the words in the box.

St. Patrick's Day	precise	perform	competition

First viewing

D. Watch the video and write down the reasons these people like Irish dancing.

Second viewing

E. Watch the video again and find the answers to these questions. You will need to make inferences from the information in the video.

1. Irish dancing is done in only a few places.   True   False
   How do you know this?

2. The girl who talks about her shoes dances a lot.   True   False
   How do you know this?

3. There are contests for Irish dancing.   True   False
   How do you know this?

After viewing

F. Talk about these questions.

1. If someone asked you, "What does Irish dancing look like?" how would you describe it?

2. Do you think people in your country would enjoy doing Irish dancing? Why? or why not? Would you like to try it?

Unit 8: Florida Keys Dolphins

Before viewing

A. Where is Florida? What are some famous places for visitors there? You are going to watch a video about travel in the Florida Keys. Find the Florida Keys on a map.

B. PAIR WORK What do you think the climate is like in the Florida Keys? What kind of plants and animals do you think you might see there? Would you like to go take a vacation in Florida? Why? or why not?

C. Check the meaning of the words in the box.

resort (n)	key	southernmost	scarce

First viewing

D. Watch the video and write down three interesting things tourists can see in the Florida Keys.

Second viewing

E. Listen for specific details. Watch again and find the answers to these questions.

1. How old is Calvin?
2. How long is the bridge?
3. What do people in Key West do every day?
4. What does the narrator recommend for an interesting trip?

After viewing

F. Talk about these questions.

1. Why do you think visitors go to the Florida Keys?
2. What is unusual about traveling in the Florida Keys?
3. What is the southernmost place in your country? Is there anything different or special there?
4. Where is the biggest (or longest) bridge in your country? Have you seen it?

Unit 9: Big Screen Comics

Before viewing

A. PAIR WORK What types of movies are the most popular now? Why do you think they are so popular? Do you like these types of movies? Why or why not?

B. Check the meanings of the words in the box.

disappointment	the public	character	hero

First viewing

C. Read the questions, then watch and take notes. Answer the questions after you watch.

1. Where did the ideas for these movies come from?
2. What are the names of some movies in the video?
3. Why do people like these movies?
4. Were all of these movies successful?

Second viewing

D. Watch again and fill in the spaces.

1. RERPORTER: For the _____ in Hollywood who take those comic books and put them on the big screen, what do you want them to know? What should they be reminded of?
   STAN LEE: Well, I think the first thing they should think of is, forget that these are comic books. These are _____, with characters. The characters have individualistic _____. The characters, when they speak, it has to be _____ dialog. It has to be believable.

2. REPORTER: Despite the risks, the payoff can be, like Spiderman, amazing. The top _____ comic-inspired films have collectively grossed nearly _____ billion dollars in the _____ —making the future, for those that will follow, look very _____.

After viewing

E. Talk about these questions.

1. How are these movies different from movies about real people?
2. Are these movies popular in your country?
3. Do you think there will be more movies like this in the future? Why or why not?

Unit 10: Skateboard Mama

Before viewing

A. PAIR WORK When you were a child, what did you do in your free time? What do you like to do now? Which things are the same, and which are different? Are any of your favorite activities dangerous? Will you stop them when you get older?

First viewing

B. Watch the video and find the answers to these questions.

1. How old is Liz?
2. When did she get her skateboard?
3. Where was she from?
4. What did she decide to do in the U.S.?

Second viewing

C. Watch the video again, and take notes about these things:

- how Liz feels about younger people
- why Liz started skateboarding
- Liz's ideas about the United States
- what older people think about Liz

After viewing

D. Talk about these questions.

1. Is skateboarding popular in your country? Have you ever tried it?
2. Why do you think Liz enjoys skateboarding so much?
3. If an elderly person in your family wanted to do something dangerous, what would you say?

Unit 11: Teaching Friendship

Before viewing

A. Check the meaning of this word: bully (n. and v.) Is bullying a problem in schools in your country?

B. PAIR WORK Who was your first good friend when you were a child? What kinds of things did you like to do together? Think back to your experiences in elementary school. Were there any children who didn't have friends? How do you think this affected them?

C. You are going to watch a video about children's problems at school. Check the meaning of the words in the box.

ignore	upset (adj) depressed	friendship	pick on

First viewing

D. Watch the video and find the information.

1. Sue Clendening is a teacher who collected information about children's _____.
2. She gave her students a _____.
3. _____ % of the children said they were often alone because no one wanted to play with them.
4. She also asked the children to name three people who most needed _____ _____.
5. To help the children, teachers began putting them _____ _____.

Second viewing

E. Why are friends important? Watch the video again and write down the ideas of these people.

1. Carla Garrity
2. the first child
3. the second child

After viewing

F. Talk about these questions.

1. In your opinion, why do some children bully others?
2. What are some good ways for shy children to make more friends?

3. What do you think will happen to these children when they grow up?

4. Should teachers try to help children with personal problems? Or is that their parents' responsibility?

Unit 12: As Seen on TV

Before viewing

A. **PAIR WORK** What kinds of things are usually advertised on TV? Do you believe the advertising? In your country, are there things sold on TV that you can't buy in stores? Have you ever bought anything like this?

B. Check the meaning of the words in the box.

commercial (n)	amazing	incredible	product

First viewing

C. Watch the video and answer these questions.

1. How would you describe the narrator's way of speaking?

2. Why do you think the narrator is speaking like this?

3. How would you describe the products in this store?

Second viewing

D. Watch again and find this information

1. the name of these stores

2. when they started

3. how many stores there are

4. what they sell

5. the name of one product

6. why these products are special

After viewing

E. Talk about these questions.

1. Do you ever buy things because you saw them on TV?

2. Do you like to watch TV commercials? Why or why not? What are some of the best/worst commercials on TV now?

3. Have you ever bought a product like the ones in the video? Did it work?

Language Summary

Understanding the English verb system

The form of any English verb is made up of two things:

1. time: present, past, future
2. aspect: simple, continuous, perfect

Time tells us when something took place. And the aspect tells us how the speaker or writer interprets the event.

Aspect	Simple	Continuous	Perfect
Time			
Present	She *goes* to school at St. Michael's.	*I'm finishing* my final paper.	John *had seen* that movie before.
Past	It *snowed* yesterday.	It *was raining* when we got home.	Steve *had already gone* home when I arrived.
Future	My son *will come* home for Christmas.	Don't come at noon. *I'll be having* lunch with Chris.	The movie *will have finished* by 8:00.

English also has an active and a passive voice.

> Mary *prepared* dinner for us tonight.
>
> Dinner *was prepared* by the time we arrived.

Uses of the –ing form

We call the *-ing* form of the verb a present participle or a gerund. As present participles they form part of the verb or adjectival phrase. As gerunds they act as nouns.

1. We use present participles in the progressive or continuous tenses:

   Present continuous: Susan is *reading*.

   Present perfect continuous: Katie has been *using* her new computer every day since she bought it.

   Past continuous: John was *studying* for his test when we came home.

   Past perfect continuous: Ron had been *studying* at the university for two semesters when he had to leave.

   Future continuous: Thirty minutes from now we will be *having* lunch at our hotel.

   Future perfect continuous: When my father retires from teaching next year he probably won't know what to do with his extra time because he will have been *working* at the university for forty years.

2. We also use present participles as adjectives:

   We took the *winding* path up the hill.

3. We can use gerunds as the subject of a sentence:

   Studying for tests is hard work.

4. We can also use gerunds as the object of certain verbs or verbs + prepositions:

   He regrets *moving* to Australia.

   I'm looking forward to *meeting* you.

More uses of the –ing form

Gerunds and infinitives can both be used after certain verbs. It is important to learn what verbs can be followed by a gerund and what verbs can be followed by an infinitive.

1. When the following verbs are followed by another verb, the second verb is always in the –ing form: **avoid, can't help, can't stand, enjoy, dislike, finish, mind, suggest**
2. When the following verbs are followed by another verb, the second verb is always in the infinitive form: **agree, choose, decide, hope, plan, prepare, seem, want**
3. The following verbs can be followed by either the –ing form or the infinitive with no difference in meaning: **hate, like, love, prefer, start**
4. The following verbs can be followed by either the –ing form or the infinitive but the meaning is not the same: **forget, remember, try**

forget + infinitive	*forget* + –ing
We use *forget* + infinitive to talk about something we did not do that we should have done.	We use *forget* + –ing (often in negative sentences) to talk about memories of things we did in the past.
remember + infinitive	*remember* + –ing
We use *remember* + infinitive to talk about something that we have to do or had to do.	We use *remember* + –ing to talk about something we did in the past.
try + infinitive	*try* + –ing
We use *try* + infinitive to talk about making an effort to do something.	We use *try* + –ing to make a suggestion or to talk about a possible solution to a problem.

Relative clauses: restrictive and nonrestrictive

Relative clauses describe a noun in the sentence. There are two kinds:

1. Restrictive clauses that answer the question "what kind?" or "which one?" providing us with essential information.
2. Nonrestrictive clauses which give us additional but nonessential information about a noun in the sentence.

Restrictive clauses are much more common in spoken language. We use the relative pronoun *who* for people and *which* or *that* for things.

The young man *who cleans the pool* has not come in two weeks.

In sentences with restrictive clauses, we can omit the relative pronouns when they are objects.

Did you like the movie *we went to*? (*that* is omitted)

Nonrestrictive clauses are usually used in written language. Since the information they offer is not essential to the meaning of the sentence we generally don't need them when speaking. In written English, we put a comma before a nonrestrictive clause and, if it comes in the middle of a sentence, we put one after it as well.

Steve O'Connor, who Karen is seeing, seems a nice person.

In sentences with nonrestrictive clauses we cannot omit the relative pronoun.

Uses of the present perfect

The present perfect connects the past to the present. It deals with past actions, but we use it when we want to know how this action affects us now.

We sometimes get confused over when to use the simple past and when to use the present perfect.

We use the simple past to talk about an event or a situation that occurred at a specific time in the past and that is now finished. We use the present perfect when we are more interested in the present results or consequences of a past action. The action is unfinished at the moment of speaking or it could still happen again.

Present perfect
It's *been raining* all day.
(It's still raining.)

Simple past
It *rained* this morning.
(It has stopped raining.)

Past perfect

When talking about past events or situations, the past perfect is used to talk about an earlier past. By combining the simple past tense with the past perfect we can set two past events in chronological order. We use the past perfect for the earlier event and usually the simple past for the second event.

Before many famous actresses *became* stars, they *had been* waitresses.

We often use time expressions like **before, after, until, by the time,** etc. also in past perfect sentences to help us clarify the order of events.

Passive voice

When we use the passive voice, we shift the emphasis of the sentence from the agent—the person or thing performing an action—to the action itself. In some passive sentences, the agent is still important and we mention it, often preceded by the word **by.** When the agent is not important, is obvious and understood by all, or is unknown to us, or when it is necessary to conceal its identity—it can be completely omitted.

New laws against pollution *have been put* into effect.

Action *has been taken* against the pollutors by the local government.

The easiest way to understand the construction of passive voice sentences is by inverting an active sentence. The object of the active sentence becomes the subject of the passive sentence.

	Subject	**Verb**	**Object**
Active:	That engineer	designed	the bridge.
Passive:	The bridge	was designed by	that engineer.

Passive voice constructions often carry a more formal tone than active sentences, which tend to be more direct. For this reason we often use the passive voice in reports, official notices, descriptions of technical and scientific phenomena, etc.

For the same reason, we must be careful not to overuse the passive voice and distance the listener / reader from the information we wish to communicate.

Conditionals

There are three main types of conditional sentences.

1. Open (or first) conditional sentences are used to talk about possible future events or situations. Depending on the action of the conditional clause, the action of the main clause may or may not take place.

    If you *study* well, you *will pass* your exams.

2. Unreal (or second) conditional sentences are used to talk about the present or the future but, unlike first conditional sentences, these express actions or situations that are improbable, hypothetical, or imaginary. It is unlikely that the condition will happen.

> If I *were* taller, I *would work* as a model.

> If people *would stop* littering, this *would be* a lovely park.

3. Unreal past (or third) conditional sentences are used to talk about things that did not happen or about situations that did not exist. These sentences deal with events completely in the past and it is now too late to change the circumstances. We usually use these third conditional sentences to express either relief or regret about past events that cannot be changed.

> If I *hadn't studied* English, I never *would have gotten* this job.

> If I *had taken* more classes last semester, I *wouldn't have had* to study during the summer.

The zero or habitual conditional

We usually feel more comfortable using the first three types of conditionals because they each display a marked contrast between the tenses and we can learn them with strict rules.

"If you do *x*, *y* will happen." or, "If I had *x*, I would *y*." or, "If I had done *x*, *y* wouldn't have happened." etc.

But conditional sentences can be more varied. There are situations in which the verbs on both sides of the comma are in the same tense.

These conditionals must be analyzed in terms of the logic of the relationship between the two parts in the sentence. They can explain habitual action or scientific fact.

> If I have time, I go to the movies.

> If water boils, steam rises.

Direct objects and complements

Transitive verbs take a direct object. The verb **to be** and some other verbs take a complement. The charts below show different types of objects and complements.

Direct objects	
Form	**Example**
1. Noun	1. Joyce teaches *aerobics* every day. (noun)
2. Pronoun	2. She enjoys *it*. (pronoun)
3. Noun Phrase	3. Joyce has *her own fitness center and a videotape*. (noun phrase)
4. Gerund Phrase	4. Her students like *exercising to music*. (gerund phrase)
5. Infinitive Phrase	5. Joyce hopes *to open another fitness center* soon. (infinitive phrase)
6. Noun Clause	6. She knows *how to make this business successful*. (noun clause)

Complements	Notes

Subject complements

1. Joyce seems *happy*.

A subject complement describes the subject.
(adjective)
An intransitive verb links the subject and its complement.

2. Joyce is *an aerobics instructor*.

A subject complement can be an adjective (1), a noun phrase (2), an infinitive phrase (3), or a (noun phrase) noun clause (4).

3. Her dream is *to have two fitness centers*.
    (infinitive phrase)

4. Fitness is *what she really believes in*.
    (noun clause)

Object complements

1. Many people consider *aerobics the best workout*.
    (dir. obj.)   (obj. comp.)

An object complement describes the direct object.
Verbs such as *consider, find, call, imagine,* and *prove,* which reflect the opinion or perception of the speaker, take noun or adjective object complements as in (1) and (2).

2. Mary finds *aerobics exhausting*.
    (dir. obj.) (obj. comp.)

3. Sports Illustrated labeled *the 80s the decade of fitness*.
    (dir. obj.)   (obj. comp.)

Verbs such as *call, label, name,* which indicate a name or label for the object, take noun object complements as in (3).
A few verbs that are followed by *as* or *for* are followed by object complements as in (4), e.g. *recognize, regard, accept, mistake, take, describe.*

4. Many people regard *the fitness craze* as a *wake-up call*.
    (dir. obj.)   (obj. comp.)

Idioms and metaphors

You cannot just learn words in isolation. Many of them come in expressions that must be learned as a group.

Idioms are among the most common expressions. They are fixed and recognized by native speakers. You can't make them up. And they use language in a metaphorical, nonliteral way.

I saw *right through him*

Money *doesn't grow on trees.*

Good for you!

Metaphors exist in all languages. You use a metaphor when you take one idea and use it for another idea.

The boy *howled* in pain.

Idioms use metaphorical language.

That man is **barking** *up the wrong tree.*

You cannot learn a language without understanding its idioms and metaphors. Everyday English is idiomatic. The metaphorical use of words is often much more common than the original meanings. By learning the literal meanings of words you can form pictures in your head that will help you guess the metaphorical or idiomatic meaning.

When I told my father about my bad grades, *he went through the roof.*

Glossary

Word	Definition
a cross between	a mix of two different things
abandon	stop using
abdomen	the belly, stomach area
acclaim	public admiration
adjust	change so that it fits
advance	an improvement
amusement	pleasure, delight, entertainment, fun
appropriately dressed	wearing clothes that are correct or suitable for the occasion
areas of conflict	the place where a war is taking place
arid	very dry
ashamed	unhappy and uncomfortable about something
baggy	very loose and wide
ban	not to allow / to forbid officially
bark	sound a dog makes
be on top form	playing, performing, or working at the best of one's ability
beating	defeating an opponent
biological weapons	bacterias or viruses used to harm or kill
blockbuster	a big surprise or great success
box office smashes	movies that are seen by thousands of people in one day
brain	the organ in the head used for thinking and feeling
brick	a block of hard clay used as building material
brief	official instructions to do something (formal word)
buddies	friends, pals
buttocks	the part of the body where one sits, the behind
canyon	a long, deep crack in the earth's surface
capacity	the greatest amount of people or things that a place can contain
capture	catch by force
casually dressed	wearing informal, relaxed clothes
catch off guard	to surprise greatly
censor	to remove parts of printed or filmed materials that are considered offensive
cliff	a high rock formation with a steep drop
Cold War	period in history when the Soviet Union and the West did not trust one another
come up against	experience or have
come up with	find or propose
confide in	to tell secrets to someone
conflict	a difference, disagreement
corrupting	to make dishonest

Word	Definition
counter-productive	not useful, damaging
courts	an area marked off for sports
crafts market	a place where hand-made things are sold
crisis	an emergency
chatter	rapid sounds made by some animals
chemical weapon	a substance made from a chemical process, used to harm or kill
chisel a plum	be very lucky (very uncommon)
degradation	loss of strength
demanded	to ask for very strongly
demonstrative	showing feelings openly, esp. affection
destruction	terrible and complete ruin
discipline	control (of mind, emotions, body)
diversification	increase in the variety of activities
documentary	a film or television program based on facts and historical records
dune	hill of sand
dynasty	a ruling family
elegant	stylish in appearance, graceful
establishing a clear distinction	clarifying the difference between two things
face up to	accept
fair-weather friends	referring to people who are one's friends only in good times
feller	very informal word for guy
field	an area of land on which sports events are played
fight against	to argue, quarrel
fire	use a gun
firearms	any of a variety of guns (pistols, rifles, machine guns, etc)
fjord	narrow area of sea which goes far into high land
for my money	in my opinion12
form a partnership	work together officially
formidable	extremely strong or powerful
geographic feature	an important part or characteristic of the landscape
get along with	understand
give a hug	embrace, the act of putting one's arms around someone
go through with	finish or complete
growl	a low sound made in anger
half-time	the break in the middle of a soccer or football game
halfway	in the middle, between two points
have a lot in common	to have the same interests, tastes, etc.
head for	follow a direction

Word	Definition
herdsman	a person who looks after animals such as sheep and goats
hips	the part of the body where the leg joins the pelvis
howl	to cry loudly
hum	to make a continuous sound of "M"
illusion	an incorrect idea of reality
indoctrinate	to teach someone that certain opinions and customs are the right ones
internal organ	the parts of an animal inside the body that have a specific function
itinerary	a travel plan, showing places to visit and transportation times
judgment	decision in a court of law
keen	strong, intense
kidneys	the organs that clean our blood and are located in the lower back near the hips
leveling the score	to score the same points as the opposing team
liver	the organ in the body that helps in digestion and cleaning the blood
lock up	close with a key
log	tree trunk that has been cut
loyal	faithful to others, esp. one's friends or country
lull	a temporary stopping of activity
lungs	the breathing organs in the chest that supply oxygen to the blood
majestic	magnificent, spectacular
mass media	television, radio, and large urban newspapers used to communicate with people daily
match	contest, game between participants
means of transport	ways to move from one place to another
mirror	glass in which you can see yourself
mission	journey
moral standards	what is commonly accepted as right or wrong
mud	mixture of water and dirt
mutual friend	a shared friend between two people
natural landmark	a natural place that is a point of interest
navel	the little hollow in our stomach area
navigation	the science of planning sea journeys
navy	a country's sailors and fighting ships with their related equipment
notion	idea
oasis	a place with trees and water in the desert
objective	not influenced by emotions or personal beliefs, fair
oblivious to	not knowing

Word	Definition
overdressed	wearing clothes that are too formal for the situation
peace processes	to apply a procedure to maintain peace
peace-keeping	to prevent the outbreak of war or rebellion
peak	the pointed top of a mountain
pelf	an informal word for money (very uncommon)
penetrate	to pass or cut a way into or through
perceivable	something you can see, hear or smell
percussion	musical instruments such as drums, cymbals, and tambourines
phenomenon	a highly unusual event or person that attracts attention
pick up	record
pistol	a small gun that can be held and shot in one hand
plain	broad area of flat land
plateau	very high, flat piece of land
platform	high structure, like a table without legs
plot	the main story in a novel or play
prayer	the act of talking to your God
project	make an image appear on a screen or surface
purr	the soft, rhythmic hum made by a happy cat
put up with	tolerate or accept
range of mountains	a group of mountains in a general area
rebel	person who resists the government
rejection	not being accepted
remote	far from where people live
resilient	able to recover one's strength quickly
resist	to remain strong against opposing forces
resolve their differences	to solve something, find a solution to a problem
reveal	provide information that has been secret
reverse	change back
revival	a reawakening, a new consciousness
rink	a place for roller skating or ice skating that has a wall or fence around it
roar	to make a loud, scary sound
rope	a thick cord used for tying or hanging things
ruled	controlled
rumble	low, powerful rolling noise
score a hat-trick	a point made in a soccer game
screenplay	the script for a movie; like a play but written for film
scriptwriter	the person who writes the words for a speaker or actor
second half	The last part of a soccer game

Word	Definition
sensationalism	real or imagined events that cause great excitement or interest
shore	sandy or rocky area next to the sea or a lake
shuttle	a vehicle that travels regularly between two places
side	group or team
snarl	to make an angry sound while showing one's teeth
soldier	a person who fights for his or her country
source	place something comes from
spear	a long, thin pole with a sharp point, used in hunting and warfare
special effects	(in film, radio, TV, etc) sights and sounds created by people to seem real, such as things disappearing, strange monsters walking around, etc
spectator	an observer of an event
spy	a person who collects secret information and reports back to his or her government
story line	the main plot in a novel or play
subjective	related to personal feeling and opinion, rather than facts
summit	the highest part of a mountain

Word	Definition
suspension	hanging
sword	a weapon with a handle and long steel blade
take a cue from	follow the example of
take things at a slower pace	to measure and enjoy a trip by taking steps
the court	place where kings, queens, or emperors live
the novelty wears off	something is no longer new or interesting
risk of	possible danger of
thighs	the part of the leg between the hip and knee
toning	increasing the firmness of . . .
troops	military personnel, especially soldiers
varying degrees of success	sometimes successfully, sometimes unsuccessfully
vast	big and wide
venue	place where an event happens
versatile	useful in many ways
wage wars	to begin and continue a quarrel
walk out on	leave or abandon
waterfalls	water falling from a high place
weapon	a tool used to harm or kill